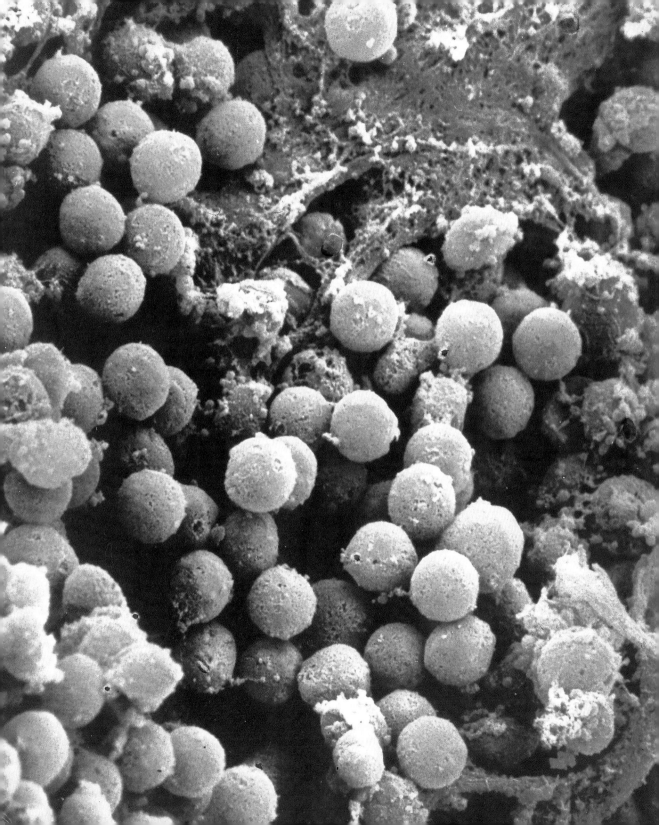

THE IMMUNE SYSTEM

Your Body's Disease-Fighting Army

Mark P. Friedlander, Jr.
&
Terry M. Phillips, Ph.D., D.Sc. (London)

 Lerner Publications Company ■ Minneapolis

Dedicated to our wives, Dorothy and Jennifer

Page two: Deep in the thymus, white blood cells become T cells, the main branch of the immune system army.

A Note on the Photographs

Many of the photographs in this book are scanning electron micrographs (SEMs) or transmission electron micrographs (TEMs). These images are magnified anywhere from 1,000 to 20,000 times. The colors in the pictures are not the actual colors but are applied afterward so that the images may be seen more easily.

Lerner Publications Company
A Division of Lerner Publishing Group
241 First Avenue North
Minneapolis, MN 55401 U.S.A.

Website address: www.lernerbooks.com

LIBRARY OF CONGRESS CATALOGING-IN-PUBLICATION DATA

Friedlander, Mark P.
    The immune system : your body's disease-fighting army / Mark P.
Friedlander, Jr. and Terry M. Phillips.
        p. cm.
    Includes index.
    Summary: Describes the immune system, its major components, and
such related topics as bacteria, viruses, parasites, vaccines, and
current research in immunology.
    ISBN 0-8225-2858-4 (alk. paper)
    1. Immune system—Juvenile literature.   [Immune system.]
I. Phillips, Terry M. II. Title.
QR181.8.F75 1998
616.07'9—dc21   97-10711

Manufactured in the United States of America
2 3 4 5 6 7 – JR – 05 04 03 02 01 00

CONTENTS

Chapter One

WHAT IS THE IMMUNE SYSTEM?

"I don't want that needle!"

"I'm sorry, but it's for your own good."

Have you ever had a conversation like that? You can probably remember being at your doctor's office and seeing a tray with various instruments lined up neatly on a clean white paper cloth. But the only thing you really noticed was that needle. You knew you were going to get a shot, or maybe two shots. And you knew the shots were going to hurt. If you had a choice, you probably would be happy to do without the shot!

The brief pain you suffered from the needle prick was well worth it, however. The shot was a **vaccination.** Vaccinations protect you from a wide range of diseases, from mumps and measles to diphtheria and polio. Some vaccinations provide life-time protection. Some vaccinations, such as the one for tetanus, require booster shots—more shots every few years or more. Others, such as a flu shot, only last for a year.

The vaccination you received helps your own natural defense mechanisms protect you better. When you understand how your **immune system** works, you'll appreciate the vaccination—and be glad that you got one.

Most of us hate getting a shot, but vaccinations help our immune systems defend against diseases.

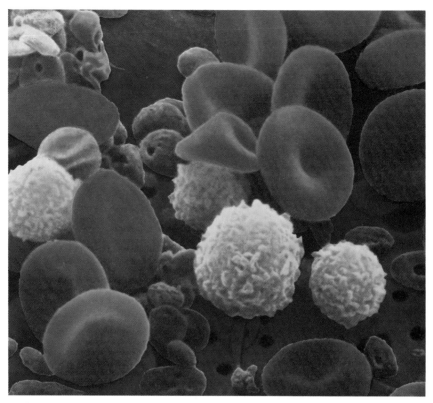

*White blood cells—the bumpy yellow spheres in this photograph—
form the main part of the immune system. The red disks are red
blood cells, and the smaller cells are platelets.*

THE IMMUNE ARMY

Your immune system is an organized army of millions and millions of white blood cells working with millions and millions of
smaller **protein** molecules called **antibodies.** The units of this
army are so small they can only be seen through a microscope.
They travel throughout your body in the rivers and streams
formed by your blood vessels, through the creeks formed by

your lymph system, and then out of the river beds and stream beds. They move between all the cells of your organs—such as your heart, lungs, liver, and brain—and the cells of your skin. All these units are highly organized, with commanders and a complex communication system.

HOW DO THEY HELP?

Every day of your life, you are awash in a sea of invisible creatures—invisible except under a microscope. These creatures are **microbes—viruses, bacteria, parasites,** and **fungi.** There are more than 250 million different types of microbes, and many of them are looking for ways to get inside your body and set up a home. These microorganisms may cause you to get sick or get

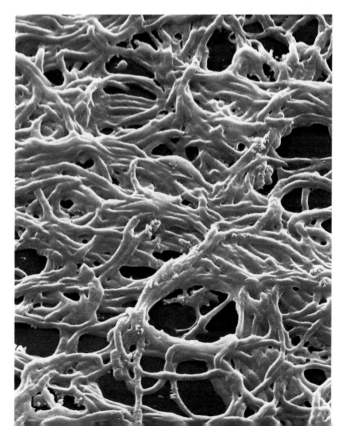

The Legionella pneumophila *bacteria—one of millions of microbes in the world—can cause fever, headache, and diarrhea in humans.*

a disease. Your immune system is designed to fight against these invaders.

Your own immune army can also make you sick. When it gets confused, the immune system begins to attack some of your own body parts. This results in what are known as **autoimmune diseases.** Multiple sclerosis and rheumatic fever, for example, are autoimmune diseases. Your immune army may also overreact to pollens, dust, certain chemicals, or some foods, causing an allergic or **hypersensitive reaction**—an itchy rash, sneezing, a stuffed-up nose, or shortness of breath.

THE THREE KEYS

Three key facts about your immune system make it special. These keys make it work.

1. *It distinguishes.* Your immune system can tell one invader from another—it distinguishes each germ from every other. For example, if a mumps virus enters your body, your white blood cells recognize it; they don't mistake it for, say, a flu virus.

2. *It remembers.* After your body has been infected with a disease-causing microbe, such as a mumps virus, your immune army will remember what it is and how to fight it. If the mumps virus shows up again, your white blood cells will strike it down quickly. The fact that your immune system has memory is the secret to vaccinations.

3. *It knows itself.* As the units of the immune system flow through your body looking for invaders, they recognize your own parts, so they will not harm them. That is why organ transplants cause problems. The immune system sees the new, transplanted organ and says, "Hey, that wasn't here before. It is not part of this body, so let's attack it."

CELLULAR AND HUMORAL IMMUNITY

The vast and complex army of the immune system is divided into two different forces. The white blood cells that travel throughout the body and attack foreign invaders wherever they are form what is called **cellular immunity.** Some of these roving units destroy any invader that does not belong in your body. Other cells attack only specific enemies. These forces make up the first line of defense.

The second, more sophisticated force is made up of antibodies. Millions of antibodies can be manufactured to fight specific invaders. Antibodies and the cells that manufacture them make up **humoral immunity.** Both forces, working together, provide the power of the immune system.

But let's not get ahead of ourselves. There's a lot to learn about the immune system. You can also discover how to make your immune system work better for you. This book will explore all this and more.

Chapter Two

HOW THE IMMUNE SYSTEM WORKS

Your skin is your body's outer line of defense against invaders. Think of your skin as a giant security blanket that stretches over your body, protecting every part of it. Just as your heart and lungs and liver are separate organs, your skin is one single, distinct organ. Your skin shields you against the microbes and environmental forces that you encounter every day.

Microorganisms enter your body either through the body's natural openings—eyes, ears, nose, mouth, anus, vagina, or urethra—or through cuts, punctures, scrapes, burns, or watery rashes. Although some chemical poisons can be absorbed through skin, no virus, bacteria, or other microbe can pass through healthy skin.

You know that you need to protect yourself from cuts and burns, but the natural openings in the body also need protection. The immune system protects these openings with tears, saliva, and other fluids. The fluids contain special chemicals that will fight any invaders trying to enter the body.

HOW THE IMMUNE SYSTEM DEVELOPS

Before you were born, while you were still in your mother's womb, your immune system began to develop. As the immune

When someone sneezes near you, bacteria or viruses can travel in the air and enter your body through your nose and mouth.

[13]

system forms, it must have a way to determine the "bad guys"—foreign invaders—from the "good guys"—the cells that make up your own body.

Cells are the basic units that make up living creatures. Humans are made of billions of cells, grouped together into tissues and organs. All of your cells come from the joining together of the cells of your mother and the cells of your father. Your cells contain genes that determine the characteristics you inherit from your parents. This genetic material is in the cell's nucleus, the control center that directs the cell's activities.

Before birth, every cell in your body is marked with a special

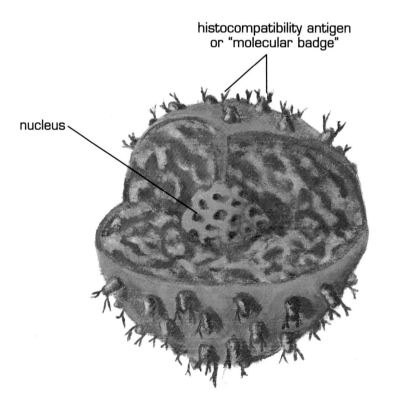

histocompatibility antigen
or "molecular badge"

nucleus

chemical badge. This badge consists of a series of molecules on the surface of the cell—the same series on each cell, so all of your cells display the same badge. The badge is called a **histo-compatibility antigen.** It marks each cell as yours. The molecules that make up the badge are unique to you—the badge is yours and yours alone. Of the billions of people on earth, each one has a different badge. Some badges are very different from yours, and others are only slightly different. But they are all different, just like your fingerprints or your own Internet access code or password.

The white blood cells and antibodies that circulate constantly through your body are like police officers with billy clubs. As they pass each cell, they tap it with the club and say, "Let me see your badge." If the cell does not have the correct badge, the police know it is "foreign," an unwanted intruder. These foreign cells are referred to as **antigens.** Antigens are targeted to be destroyed. The marker badge that each antigen displays is its own molecular identification, or series of molecules.

When you were born, your immune system was not quite ready to take on the sea of germs we all live in. A baby is protected as much as possible by the sanitary conditions her parents provide for her. Milk from the mother's breasts also provides immune protection. Antibodies from the mother's immune system are in the milk and help the baby fight germs.

Deep within the soft marrow of the big bones of your legs and arms and clavicle, or collar bone, important cells called **stem cells** produce millions and millions of different types of cells every day—red blood cells, platelets, and white blood cells. Red blood cells carry food and oxygen to all the other cells of your body. Platelets help cuts and wounds heal. White blood cells form your immune system army.

Antigens—The Triggers

An antigen is any substance that triggers an immune system attack. It can be a living invader, such as a microbe, or it can be a chemical invader, such as a food or household product. Some substances, such as nylon, Teflon, the plastic used in artificial blood vessels, and the steel of a hypodermic needle are non-antigenic. In other words, these materials will not cause an immune response.

Penicillin is not antigenic to most people, but to those who are allergic to penicillin, it is highly antigenic. This is also true of the oil from the poison ivy plant, as well as many household products.

All viruses are antigenic to almost everybody. Bacteria and other microbial invaders are antigenic to some and not to others.

Antigens create problems in blood transfusions. Blood is typed by antigenic characteristics. For instance, Type A blood has its own molecular antigenic badge, while Type B has a different badge. Type AB has antigens of both, while Type O has no antigens. A person with Type A blood cannot receive Type B or Type AB blood without invoking a violent immune response. A Type A person can receive blood from another Type A or the neutral Type O without an immune response.

White blood cells take many forms. Each type does a different job. Millions of white blood cells flow through your body. White blood cells known as **polymorphonuclear** cells or **polys** form the first line of defense. Polys meet every invader and attempt to destroy it. They do not focus on a single microbe, but rather act as general guard warriors, attacking all foreign cells. This general defense is aided by chemicals called **interferons** and by body fluids such as tears, saliva, and sweat.

If the polys can't destroy the invader immediately, they call upon the other frontline white blood cells called **macrophages.** Macrophages not only fight the enemy invaders, but they also act as messengers. They bite off a chunk of an invader and carry it back to other white blood cells so they can identify the invader and organize a response.

Macrophages flow throughout the body, especially around the skin cells so that they can deal with germs as soon as they enter the body. Sharing the task of guarding the gates are other white blood cells, or **leukocytes.** (All white blood cells are leukocytes.) Like macrophages, leukocytes challenge microbes in the first stage of an invasion.

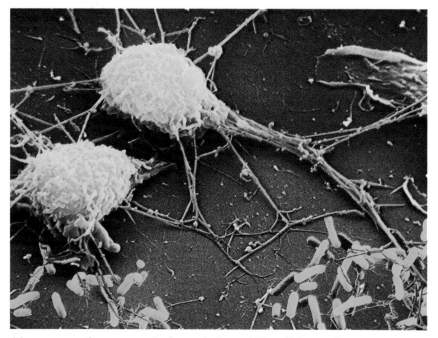

Two macrophages attack the rod-shaped E. coli *bacteria.*

The main branch of the immune system army is the group of white blood cells known as **lymphocytes.** After they're manufactured by the stem cells, some lymphocytes are carried to the **thymus,** a gland under the breastbone. The thymus is large during childhood, but it becomes smaller as you get older. In the thymus, lymphocytes go through a training center and come out as **T cells.** (All these name changes can be confusing, but T cells are still lymphocytes.)

One way to understand this transformation is by imagining that the immune system soldiers are going through boot camp training exercises. As they do, they become more and more specialized. After passing through the training center of the thymus, the T cells have been divided into four basic types: **helper T cells, suppressor T cells, killer (effector) T cells,** and **natural killer (NK) cells.** Both types of killer cells are the basic fighting forces—they directly attack antigens. The helper cells, sometimes called inducer cells, and the suppressor cells become the officers and generals of the army. They give orders to the young warriors about how to fight the invaders. When the generals receive a report that an invader has overwhelmed the macrophages, the helper T cells and the suppressor T cells determine how many killer cells and other immune units to send into battle. The helper cells always want to send too many, while the suppressor cells never want to send enough. Together, they arrive at the correct balance.

When the killer cells are sent to fight, they seek out the bacteria or other antigen, surround it, and destroy it. The killer cells are armed with chemicals known as **enzymes.** When the killer cells find bacteria, they use the enzymes like an electric drill. They drill a hole in the shell of the bacterium, causing the insides of the bacterium to pour out, the way water would

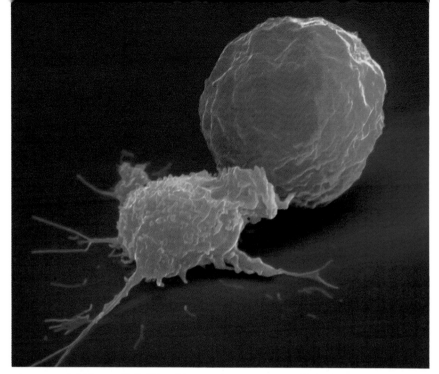

A natural killer cell (NK cell) attacks a cancer cell (colored orange).
The NK cell is about to engulf and destroy the cancer cell.

stream from a water balloon if you punched a hole in it. When that fluid—which is really more like Jell-O than water—comes out of the bacteria, other white blood cells called **phagocytes** rush in to clean up the mess.

When the commanding committee of white blood cells is not working together, problems develop. For example, the virus known as **HIV,** the cause of **AIDS,** attacks and destroys helper T cells. The committee becomes unbalanced, and not enough killer cells are sent to stop invaders. People with AIDS often get diseases like pneumonia, caused by a bacteria. The bacteria would be destroyed if the immune system were working properly.

The commanding committee also can call into action another type of white blood cell, the **B cells.** When white blood cells are needed as B cells, they are sent to a different boot camp, in the bone marrow. Antibodies are the main weapon of your immune system. An ordinary B cell manufactures antibodies slowly. When a lot of antibodies are needed to fight an invader, the B cells mature into **plasma cells,** large cell factories that make antibodies very fast.

It takes about one to three weeks for the B cells to set up their plasma cell factories and produce the specific antibodies needed to destroy an attacking microbe.

ANTIBODIES

Antibodies are molecules of protein that are shaped like a Y. At the end of each arm of the Y is a clawlike receptacle. Each claw is shaped to fit one specific biological (plant or animal) invader, such as a virus, bacteria, fungus, or parasite. These biological invaders, or antigens, have their own specific molecular badges, just as your cells do. When an antigen enters your body, antibodies seek it out. There is a specific antibody for every antigen.

Because each antibody will fit only one antigen, the claws of the antibody will only lock onto an enemy invader with a matching molecular marker or badge. The antibody and antigen are like two pieces of a puzzle that fit together.

Because producing antibodies takes a lot of energy, our bodies only use them for the major body invaders. No antibodies are produced to attack nonliving things that enter your body, such as wood splinters.

Each antibody performs another task as well. Not only does it find an invader with a matching badge, but it also inspects the body cell that is being attacked. It determines if the cell—whether it is a cell in your nose being attacked by a cold virus or a cell in your lungs being attacked by Legionnaires' disease

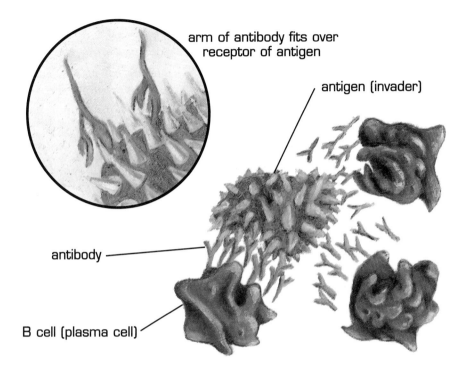

arm of antibody fits over receptor of antigen

antigen (invader)

antibody

B cell (plasma cell)

bacteria—belongs to you. If the cell has your marker on it, the antibody will not attack it. If the cell is foreign—it does not have your marker—then the antibody will attack it.

You may remember that when a macrophage faces an enemy it cannot handle, it carries a fragment from the invader back to the T cells. It does this by surrounding the entire antigen, dissolving most of it, and carrying back molecular fragments of it to the helper and suppressor T cell committee for examination. If the examination tells them that antibodies are needed, then the antigen fragments are presented to the B cells so they can begin manufacturing antibodies. The antibodies will have the same molecular marker as the antigen, and they will find and destroy any cells with that marker.

Antibody Types

All antibodies are not exactly the same. Each of the five basic types of antibodies has a slightly different assembly of molecules that form a Y shape. They are classified by Greek letters. Translated into English, they are G, A, M, D, and E. The symbol for antibodies is "Ig" (which stands for *immunoglobulin*). So the designations for the five types of antibodies are IgG, IgA, IgM, IgD, and IgE.

IgG is the main antibody. It races through the body, in and out of organs and blood vessels.

IgA is found in and around all wet surfaces, such as saliva, tears, intestinal fluids, and breast milk.

IgM is the largest antibody. It remains in the blood vessels, providing a general defense against invaders while the more specialized IgG antibodies are being made.

IgD is found on the surface of certain B cells to help search for invaders.

IgE locks on to mast cells and basophils to release histamine and bring in certain white blood cells to fight parasites and allergens.

Millions of antibodies are sent to battle. They lock on to the invaders. Then they send signals to units called **complement.** These units are enzymes that help kill the invader by dissolving it.

While most antibodies are fighting off invaders, some antibody-producing B cells are sent to the **lymph nodes.** Lymph nodes, or lymph glands, are located throughout your body. Within the lymph nodes are thousands of B cells ready to produce specific antibodies upon demand. These antibodies are for viruses or bacteria that were previously introduced into your body.

When you get a vaccination, a small dose of dead or inactive bacteria or virus is injected into your arm. For example, you might get a vaccination for measles. The immune system processes the information about the virus. Your body makes antibodies for measles, and the B cells are sent to the lymph nodes. If the measles virus enters your body again a year later, your immune system does not have to go through the process of gathering the information needed to make antibodies. Because of the vaccination, the memory of the measles antibody is stored in the B cells in your lymph nodes. The B cells can instantly produce the antibodies, and the measles virus is destroyed before it can take control of your cells. You have specific protection, or **immunity.** Immunity means that the second time your body is exposed to an antigen, the immune response will be stronger.

The immunological memory stored in the B cells in your lymph nodes is like a computer's memory. The B cells save the information about an invader in an immunological directory. Just as you might click your mouse a few times to open a computer game, your immune system can open the B-cell "file" about a certain invader to launch an immediate antibody response.

Antibodies remain in the body for only about three weeks. They are flushed away to make room for new antibodies. That's why the stored B cells with memory are important.

THE TRANSPORTATION SYSTEM

If you are wondering how the white blood cells travel through the body, you have asked a good question. It's white-water rafting all the way! More correctly, red-blood rafting part of the

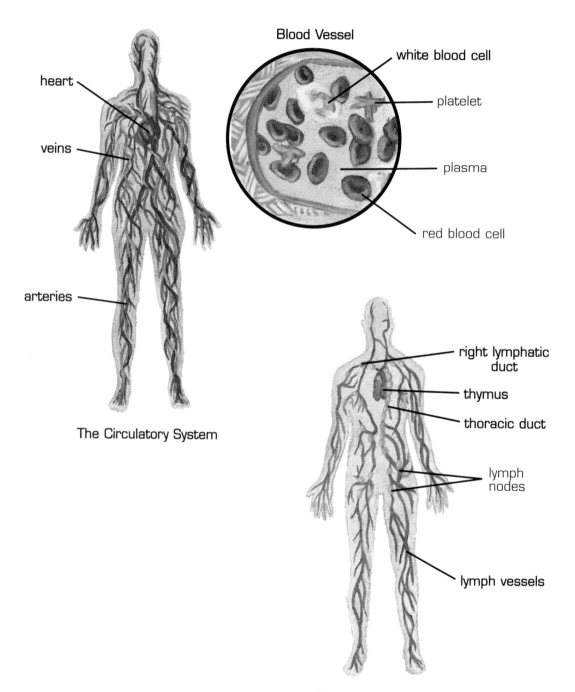

Blood Vessel

white blood cell

platelet

plasma

red blood cell

heart

veins

arteries

The Circulatory System

right lymphatic duct

thymus

thoracic duct

lymph nodes

lymph vessels

The Lymphatic System

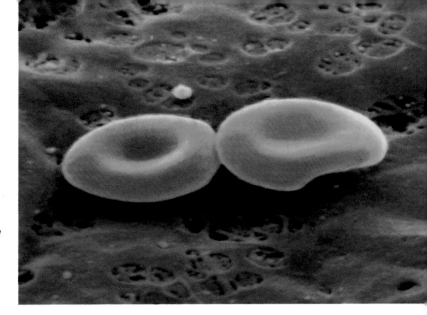

Two red blood cells travel through a capillary. Nutrients move from the red blood cell into other cells through the small indented holes in the wall of the capillary.

way, followed by **lymph**-fluid rafting the rest of the way. Just like red blood cells, white blood cells flow in the rivers and streams of blood—through arteries to the capillaries. Then the white blood cells part company from the red blood cells. From the capillaries, white blood cells move into the lymph fluid in the **lymph vessels.** Lymph fluid is clear, almost like water. It is a special type of blood that transports white blood cells only. The lymph fluid is not only a transportation system, but it also provides nutrients for the white blood cells.

While the red blood cells carry carbon dioxide, a waste product of digested food, and other waste back to the lungs to be exhaled out of the body, the white blood cells move through the lymph system. The white blood cells then flow out of the lymph vessels and around all the body cells, returning in the lymph fluids back into the blood at the thoracic duct, a spot in the arteries in the neck. Some of the white blood cells stop at lymph nodes, where they stay in case they are called to action by the immune system commanders. Lymph nodes are like inspection stations where cells and materials are examined and where a reserve of white blood cells is kept. Swollen lymph nodes are often a sign of infection, like the way lymph nodes in your neck become swollen when you have a sore throat.

THE IMMUNE SYSTEM IN ACTION

Let's take a look at how all these different parts of the immune system work together when, for example, you cut yourself. A cut in your skin causes a reaction from your immune system. The kind of reaction depends on the kind of cut. If a doctor in a hospital operating room makes a surgical cut in an area of your skin that has been sterilized (cleaned so no living organisms are present), the skin will become red and tender. But only a small number of white blood cells and platelets will come to the site, where they will find almost no invading bacteria. The platelets will seal off the stitched-up incision with a scab. Then the white blood cells begin removing dead cells as part of the healing process. This will happen quickly.

If you are working in the garden and prick your finger on a rose thorn, bacteria are at once injected under your skin. Your skin will swell up and turn red. The first line of defense, the polys, the macrophages, and the leukocytes, surround the invading bacteria, destroy them, then cart them away. In a day or two, the redness will be gone.

If, however, you gash your hand and cut all the way through your skin to draw blood, then a large number of bacteria will enter through the skin. Your immune system will sound a general alarm and call to action many different types of white blood cells. Not only will the polys, the macrophages, and the leukocytes take part in the attack, but the macrophages will also report the invasion to the T-cell command center. The command

Members of the Immune System

MEMBER	FUNCTION
MACROPHAGE	The first white blood cell to encounter a foreign invader (antigen) and take news of the attack to T cells. Kills antigen at the invasion site. Presents antigen to T and B cells. Helps clean up after an immunological response.
POLYMORPHONUCLEAR CELL (POLY)	Cleans up after an immunological response
T CELL	Lymphocyte responsible for cellular immunity. Special T cells regulate immune reactions.
HELPER T CELL	T cell that promotes immunity by sending out troops to fight invaders
SUPPRESSOR T CELL	T cell that suppresses immunity by calling back the invader-fighting troops
KILLER (EFFECTOR) T CELL	T cell that attacks invaders
NATURAL KILLER CELL	T cell that attacks invaders
B CELL	Lymphocyte responsible for humoral immunity. Produces antibodies.
ANTIBODIES	Protein molecules that can kill invaders
COMPLEMENT	Series of proteins that help antibodies kill invaders. Act as chemical messengers, signaling macrophages and polys to come to the site of battle and clean up the debris.

center will then send killer T cells to the site. They will also alert the B cells to start making antibodies. The cut will become dark red and painful.

If the garden where you cut your hand contains manure-enriched dirt, that poses an extra danger. One of the bacteria entering through the cut in your hand could be *Clostridium tetani,* the bacterium that causes the disease tetanus. Tetanus bacteria live in many types of dirt, in rust, and especially in manure.

You could have a really serious problem, or not so serious. Did you have a tetanus shot? If you did not have a tetanus vaccination, those bacteria would quickly overwhelm your white blood cells. Within a few weeks you would become depressed and have a headache. Then your jaw and throat muscles would tighten, and it would be hard for you to breathe. You could die. But if you did have a tetanus shot, your immune system, aided by the **vaccine,** would immediately overwhelm the tetanus bacteria and destroy them. Booster shots are given regularly to keep the tetanus vaccine up to date. Even if you hadn't had a booster shot, by getting a tetanus booster within a day of cutting yourself, you would be able to destroy all of the tetanus invaders. That's because the tetanus bacteria grow slowly, and the booster creates a fast response. By bedtime, only a few of the invaders would remain, but the cut would still be red and sore as white blood cells carted off the debris of battle and your tissues began to repair themselves.

Quickly washing dirt from a cut helps your immune system. This prevents additional bacteria from gaining entrance into your body. Plain cold tap water works well, if it is running in a constant stream. Public drinking water is purified and contains only a small number of bacteria. Flowing water is a good cleanser, because bacteria are easily carried away in flowing fluids.

A gentle wipe with clean cotton soaked with alcohol or another disinfectant also removes bacteria, reducing the chance of greater infection.

Burns also allow bacteria to enter your body. A burn destroys the outer layer of skin and allows the lymph fluid to seep through the burned area. When this fluid pools on your skin, it creates a great place for germs to grow. Lymph fluid is rich in food materials normally used to feed white blood cells, but also very appealing to bacteria. At the same time, because a burn seals the blood vessels and lymph vessels in the area, the rivers and streams that normally carry your army of white blood cells to the battle zone become blocked. This gives the bacteria a head start and makes fighting infection harder for your immune system.

A minor burn quickly blisters, providing a natural shield to stop any further bacterial invasion. That is why you should not puncture a blister on a burn. The skin covering the blister protects you.

A third-degree burn—a really serious kind of burn—penetrates all the layers of your skin right down to muscle. The deep burn holes trap bacteria, and infection is likely. The shock of a burn also weakens your immune army functions. Often, seriously burned people must lie in a hospital bed with their damaged skin uncovered, which helps the skin scab over naturally. These people are usually kept apart from all visitors to keep the natural bacteria that live on a visitor's clothes or skin from seeking haven in the unprotected areas of burned skin.

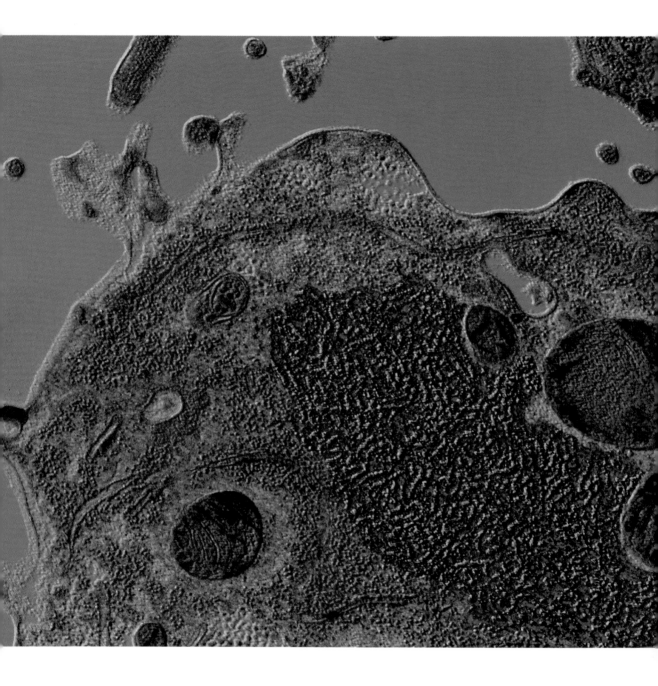

Chapter Three

THE BODY INVADERS

We have explained how the immune system works by referring to the "body invaders." But this reference is not as precise as it should be. The four basic types of body invaders or germs are viruses, bacteria, parasites, and fungi. Your immune system responds to each type in a different way.

VIRUSES

A virus is the smallest and simplest of all life forms. Viruses are so small they cannot be seen with an ordinary microscope. Only after the development of the electron microscope was it possible to see viruses. An electron microscope uses an electron beam instead of a beam of light to create an enlarged image of a small object. The electron beam relays the image to a TV screen to allow you to see the object. The image on screen is many thousands of times the actual size of the object.

Just how small is a virus? More than a million viruses could fit on the head of a pin. If you imagine that a bacterium, which you cannot see except with a microscope, was the size of a football, then a virus would be the size of a grain of sand.

There are thousands of different viruses. They come in many shapes. The most usual shapes are balls and cylinders. If you think of a virus as a soccer ball, the outside is a protein shell,

This picture may look like a landscape from another planet, but it's actually a cell infected with the measles virus, magnified 20,000 times. The green structures in the red area are the measles viruses.

and the inside is filled with a strandlike material known as **nucleic acid** or **RNA.**

A virus is inert—by itself, it can do nothing. It can't move or multiply. To recreate itself, a virus seeks a living host. Then it travels in the bloodstream or lymph streams of the host. It is carried in fluids flowing from the host. It floats through the air in droplets coughed or sneezed from a host.

A virus can enter your body through any opening in your body. A cold or flu virus usually enters through the nose or mouth. These viruses are specialized to attack cells in your nose and mouth. That's why a cold or flu affects your nose and throat first.

Once a virus gets inside a living thing, whether human, animal, or plant, it travels in the blood and lymph of humans or animals or the sap of plants until it finds a cell that it is designed to fit. Different viruses attack different parts of your body. Some viruses, such as cold and flu viruses, target the nose and throat, while others, such as polio viruses, strike cells in the nervous system. When the virus finds its target cell, it fixes itself to the outside, then finds or dissolves a way through the wall of the cell and slides into it. Inside, the virus sheds its own shell and takes over the cell's **DNA** structure—the part of the cell that determines what the cell will do. By altering the DNA, the virus turns the invaded cell into a manufacturing plant. It makes hundreds, then thousands of viruses, each identical to the original virus.

Because of the way viruses invade cells, a disease caused by a virus usually develops fast. Within a seven-hour period, a virus can clone itself from one virus into 10,000 viruses. This rapid development is what makes antibody memory so important. If antibodies are quickly called to action upon the first sighting of

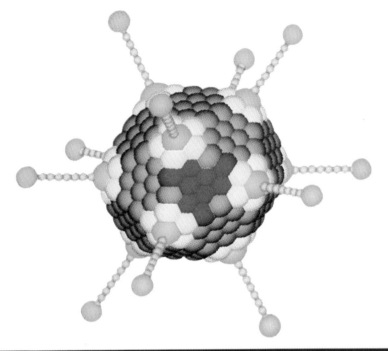

(Top) *A computer model shows the molecular structure of an adenovirus, one of the viruses that causes the common cold.* (Bottom) *HIV viruses bud from an infected T cell (at bottom, colored red and yellow). Four viruses are seen at different stages of forming. New HIV viruses get their molecular coats from the T-cell membrane (green). At left, a new, free-floating virus will move into another T cell and take it over.*

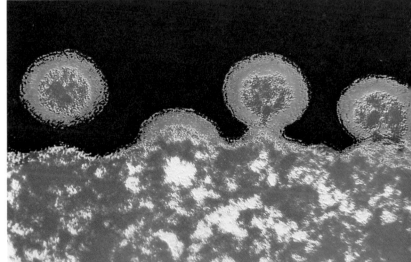

a viral invader, the host can eliminate the virus before it has a chance to multiply. After the virus has multiplied, it can take many days for your immune system to manufacture enough antibodies to defeat the virus.

Chicken pox, measles, and mumps are three childhood diseases caused by viruses. These diseases are highly contagious. The viruses spread from child to child through touch or in the air. Most kids get vaccinations for these diseases.

A wide range of infections are called "a cold." The common cold is a virus, but the throat and chest infections that accompany the cold can be bacterial. While your immune system is using energy to fight off the cold-causing virus, it is often easier for bacteria to get a foothold. Because the viruses and other infections are all different, no vaccine has been developed to give protection from the cold.

The flu (influenza) is also a virus. Flu viruses usually originate in animals or birds. Each flu virus has a slightly different-shaped shell. The different shells produce different types of flu. Every year brings different flu viruses. They mutate, new viruses emerge, and more than one type arrives at once. Because the flu virus changes each year, an effective vaccine against all types of flu has not been developed. That is why a different flu shot is offered each year.

One of the weapons available to your immune army to fight viruses is a group of proteins known as interferons. When a virus attacks, interferons are sent to the invasion site to slow the enemy down by halting its ability to multiply. While interferons hold the viruses in slow motion, the white blood cell commanders assemble their armies and send killer T cells and antibodies to begin a full-scale attack. Interferons can also stimulate T cells to multiply, increasing the total immune attack.

BACTERIA

Most bacteria are single-celled organisms that are encased in a hard coat. They are shaped like balls, rods, or coils. They move through fluids by means of tiny, hairlike fingers known as flagella. Bacteria are everywhere. Many bacteria are helpful to humans. For example, bacteria living in your intestines help you digest food. But other bacteria cause disease.

Bacteria, like viruses, enter the body through natural openings such as the mouth or nose. Bacteria also enter through cuts and burns.

While a virus kills body cells by invading them and using them to produce more viruses, bacteria kill cells by releasing a toxin—a poison—as they eat food products intended for your

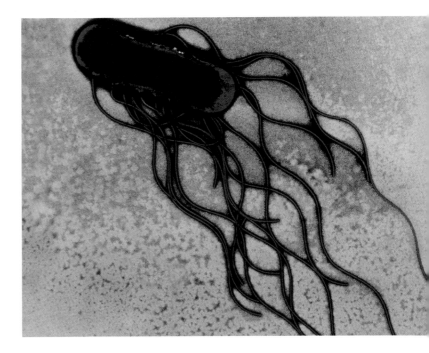

A salmonella bacterium with long flagella

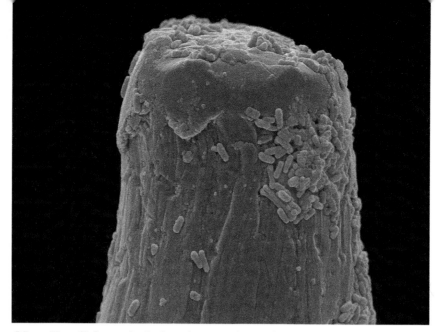

Many E. coli *bacteria (colored orange) can fit on the head of a pin.*

cells. As blood passes through your stomach and intestines, red blood cells pick up food—proteins, carbohydrates, fats, vitamins, and minerals—to deliver to all your cells. Red blood cells are like the pizza delivery guys of your body.

When bacteria arrive, they intercept the delivery guys, take the food from them, and start gorging themselves. In the process, they create waste. This waste is poisonous to the surrounding body cells. The result is cell death.

Bacteria cause a wide range of diseases, including pneumonia, whooping cough, tuberculosis, typhoid fever, and tetanus. Food poisoning is caused by bacteria such as salmonella.

Bacteria may attack specific body organs or move throughout your entire body. Each type of bacteria releases a different poison, resulting in different diseases.

Bacterial infections can be treated with medicines called antibiotics. Penicillin is a familiar antibiotic. Penicillin fools bacteria. Penicillin molecules mimic the shape and form of certain parts of protein molecules, the food for hungry bacteria. While bacteria can be dangerous, nobody ever said they were smart. The bacteria mistake the penicillin for their protein dinner, eating the penicillin until they are full. There's no nutrition for bacteria in penicillin, but they get too full to gobble up the protein they need to thrive. They literally die of starvation.

PARASITES

Some parasites are one-celled creatures similar to bacteria. Others, such as worms, are multicelled creatures. But while a bacterium is encased in a single rigid shell, a parasite has a soft shell. Because of this, parasites can move around more easily inside the human body.

Parasites come in many sizes and shapes and cause many different kinds of reactions. Single-cell parasites called **protozoa,** which produce malaria and other diseases, and larger parasites such as tapeworms are animal parasites. Fungi, yeasts, and ringworm (not a worm at all) are parasitic plants.

Parasites give the immune system a rough time. When a malaria-carrying mosquito bites a victim by stabbing its stinger nose into the person's skin, it injects protozoa into the bloodstream. Normally, white blood cells and antibodies would destroy any invader, but the protozoa immediately invade the red blood cells and hide inside their protective shells. White blood cells searching for invaders cannot find the protozoa because of their hiding place. The malaria parasite then destroys the invaded red blood cells. Not enough red blood cells are available to carry oxygen and food to other body cells. People suffering from malaria become weak and often feverish.

The trypanosome parasite, which causes a disease called

This long tapeworm looks like something out of a nightmare. (Unfortunately, it's real!)

sleeping sickness, enters the body from the bite of the tsetse fly, an insect found in some parts of Africa. As soon as the B cells manufacture antibodies to attack the trypanosome, it changes its molecular markers. The immune system thinks a new invader has entered and develops a whole new battery of antibodies. The victim's immune system weakens, bringing on fatigue and, eventually, death.

Parasites are much more complex than viruses or bacteria. Physicians must use powerful chemicals to kill or injure parasites before the immune system can recognize them and launch an effective attack. Different chemicals are used for different types of parasites.

FUNGI

The fourth invader is fungi. The fungi that cause diseases in humans are parasitic plants. They enter your body or live on your skin. As plants, fungi have a shell exterior, rigid and protective like tree bark or the stem of a flower. The fungal invaders are usually single celled and cylinder shaped. As they grow into colonies of single-celled plants, their thin, threadlike tentacles weave between cells, spreading damage. Your immune system can do little to defeat fungi, because their shells do not have a protein marker on the surface to alert the white blood cells.

Athlete's foot, yeast infection, ringworm, thrush, and certain lung diseases are caused by fungi. Various bacteria in your skin help destroy fungi. In addition, medications called fungicides and some antibiotics can destroy fungal invaders. After fungicides damage the shell of the fungi, the immune system can then attack and destroy the interior of the fungus growth.

ORGAN TRANSPLANTS

Normal human cells can also become foreign invaders. When an organ such as a liver is transplanted (moved) from one person to another, cells from the transplanted organ are seen as enemy invaders by the immune system of the person receiving the organ. The cells of the transplanted organ set off an immunological attack. Killer T cells and antibodies rush to the site, causing organ rejection, and the organ dies. Physicians solve this problem in part with medicines that suppress, or slow down, the immune system.

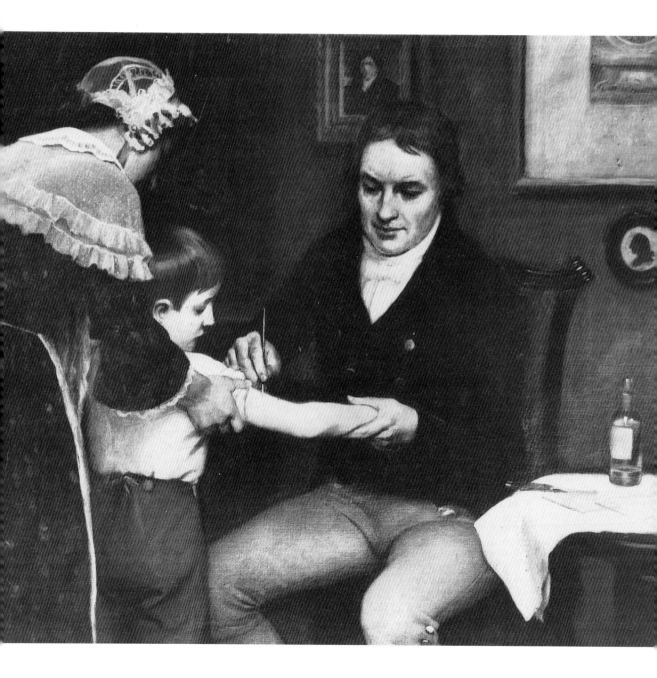

Chapter Four

VACCINATIONS: HELPING THE IMMUNE SYSTEM

Vaccinations are the medical miracle by which we help our immune systems do a better job. Vaccinations give the immune system a boost so that the body can fight a disease.

The story of vaccinations begins with smallpox. Throughout the Middle Ages (A.D. 500 to 1500), smallpox epidemics swept through Asia, Africa, and Europe, killing thousands of people. One out of every three children was likely to die from smallpox. European explorers carried this terrible disease to America.

A victim of smallpox would first suffer intense pain, high fever, and chills, followed by an angry rash of hundreds of pimples. These pimples would fill with pus and then scab over. Hands and feet would begin to swell while the virus attacked internal organs and peeled away skin. Many of the victims died. Those who survived were permanently pockmarked.

Smallpox was caused by a virus that spread from person to person through droplets in the air. But at that time, no one knew anything about bacteria or viruses.

In the spring of 1796, an English doctor, Edward Jenner, made a remarkable observation. He noticed that although smallpox epidemics spread through towns and villages, farm children who lived around cows and who caught a mild disease known as cowpox never caught smallpox. These children

Dr. Edward Jenner performed the first vaccination on eight-year-old James Phipps in 1796.

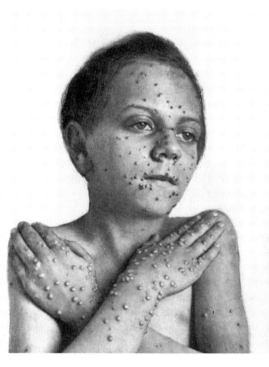

Smallpox blisters cover a child who had the disease in 1915.

seemed to possess some magical protection—they were **immune** to smallpox.

Jenner also noticed that country girls who got cowpox from milking cows often had pockmarks on their hands, where the cowpox blisters had been. These pockmarks looked like the pockmarks on the faces of smallpox victims who had survived. From this observation he reasoned that the cause of the disease was connected with the pus in the blisters.

Jenner had also heard of a technique used in Asia. A smallpox blister was scratched with a sharpened stick and then the same stick was used to scratch the skin of a healthy person. This produced a "small" case of smallpox—the person got the disease but did not die from it. Moreover, the person was prevented from getting smallpox again.

One day Jenner performed a dangerous experiment. He found a country girl who had cowpox and punctured one of the watery cowpox blisters on her wrist with a needle. Then, using the same needle, he scratched the cowpox fluid into the skin of a healthy boy, James Phipps. Several weeks later, he injected James with the watery pus from one of his patients who had smallpox. Amazingly, the boy did not catch smallpox. Jenner tried again to infect James Phipps with smallpox, but James was immune.

Jenner was criticized by other doctors for putting James Phipps's life in danger. But the doctors had to admit that Jenner's experiment was a success.

Jenner called his new procedure *vaccinia,* from the Latin word for cow—*vacca.* News of the success of the vaccinia spread. Doctors began vaccinating people to prevent smallpox. Two hundred years later, the disease has been wiped out from the world.

The word *vaccination* became widely used at the end of the 19th century, as a result of the work of French scientist Louis Pasteur. His studies of bacteria led to the development of methods to weaken microbes in the laboratory. He then injected the weakened microbes into animals to create protection against diseases such as anthrax in sheep and cholera in chickens. In 1881, Pasteur began work on a vaccine to prevent rabies, a fatal disease spread by the bite of a rabies-infected animal. Four years later, he had a chance to test his vaccine. A boy named Joseph Meister was bitten by a rabid dog. His parents came to Pasteur and begged him to help. Pasteur had never tested the vaccine on a person, but he and Joseph's parents knew that without help, the boy would die. Happily, the vaccination was successful and Joseph did not contract the deadly disease. By the early 1900s, vaccination was a familiar term.

From those beginnings, similar approaches have been used to create many vaccines. Vaccines protect us from a wide range of diseases, both viral and bacterial, including polio, measles, mumps, rabies, typhus, Rocky Mountain spotted fever, diphtheria, whooping cough, and tetanus. And more vaccines are being developed.

How Vaccinations Work

Imagine that a classmate of yours has the mumps but doesn't know it, and comes to school. Mumps is caused by a virus and is highly contagious. The mumps virus is spread by touching or is passed through the air in a cough or sneeze. If you hadn't had a mumps vaccination, you would very likely catch the mumps. But if you had had the vaccination, you would not get the disease.

When a mumps virus enters your body, it is met by the white blood cells called macrophages. These cells report back to the T-cell committee, composed of the helper cells and the suppressor cells. These cells mobilize more troops to fight the invading virus, which grows fast. The next group of white blood cells called into action are the B cells, which in turn form plasma cells. The plasma cells manufacture mumps antibodies. The antibodies rush to the mumps viruses and destroy them. But, like many viruses, the mumps viruses multiply very fast, so you will suffer all the symptoms of mumps before the B cells can manufacture enough antibodies to defeat the virus. You will have the mumps for several days before your body makes enough antibodies to overcome the virus. But once the mumps virus has been destroyed and the disease cured, the antibody-producing cells will retire to the lymph nodes and become part of your immunological memory.

When a new mumps virus invades, your immune system can move into action immediately. Since the mumps antibodies are already in the B-cell memory, the plasma cells can instantly produce new mumps antibodies to overwhelm the mumps virus before it can multiply. Millions of antibodies for mumps destroy the invaders before there is any physical sign of the disease. This is immunity.

A vaccination artificially creates the same action. A vaccine contains a small amount of the virus that causes the disease the vaccine is intended to prevent. When it is injected into your body, it triggers the immune system into producing antibodies for that virus.

Vaccinations use two different approaches. One type uses small amounts of live viruses. The virus has been weakened and altered so it will not cause a full-blown case of the disease but will produce a good antibody response. The second type of vaccination uses killed viruses. A killed virus won't cause disease, but the antigenic characteristics of even a dead virus create the antibody response necessary to provide immunity.

In 1954, Dr. Jonas E. Salk used killed polio viruses to produce the first vaccination against polio. But the killed virus produced a response that did not last long in immunological memory, so periodic booster shots were needed. Later, in 1961, Dr. Albert B. Sabin developed a weakened live virus vaccine for polio. The live-virus vaccine produced a stronger response and provided lifelong immunity.

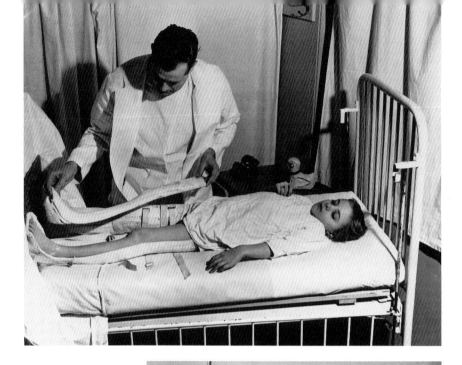

(Above) *Children with polio often had to wear braces or use a wheelchair, because the disease weakened or paralyzed their legs.* (Right) *Dr. Jonas Salk became a hero when he developed the first vaccine against polio in 1954.*

Different vaccines have different periods of effectiveness. Some require booster shots. That's because the immune system reacts differently to different microorganisms. Some invaders naturally produce a stronger antigenic response. The stronger the response, the more likely it is that your body will store B cells in memory.

SOME BAD NEWS

Many of the diseases prevented by vaccinations are the so-called childhood diseases, such as mumps and measles. In children, these diseases are usually fairly mild. The same diseases in an adult are quite another thing, however. These infections attack organs that are not developed in children but are in adults. For an adult, mumps is a serious disease. If a woman gets German measles when she is pregnant, she risks losing her baby.

In the past, epidemics of mumps and measles commonly swept through schools. In recent years, these diseases are not as likely to occur during childhood as they were in the past, because many children have had vaccinations. Thus, an unvaccinated child can reach adulthood without any protection against the childhood diseases. Adults who were not vaccinated for them are at risk.

WHEN VACCINES DON'T WORK

Some diseases defy vaccinations. Every year the public is alerted to the need for a flu shot. Why can't we get one flu shot that will protect us for our whole lives? The reason is that flu viruses constantly change their outer coat—their molecular marker. A vaccine to protect against the Asian Type A flu virus will not protect against Hong Kong Type B flu. Each year, the prevailing flu virus is different from the type that spread the year before.

Every year, public health officials must provide their best guesses about which flu virus will attack the next flu season. Based on these guesses, a flu vaccine is manufactured. If the health officials guess correctly, many people will be protected. If they guess wrong, the vaccinations will not help.

Many parasites constantly change their antigenic characteristics, which means that an antibody against the parasite will be ineffective after it changes its antigen. It's difficult or impossible to make effective vaccines against these parasites.

VACCINES OF THE FUTURE

While vaccines are generally considered safe and effective, there are side effects. Some side effects can be mild, such as fever and a sore arm, while other, less common, side effects can be serious, requiring immediate medical attention. On rare occasions, a weakened virus can cause disease.

Scientists are working to develop vaccines that are safer and do not have side effects. Synthetic (artificial) vaccines can be made using a technique called genetic engineering. Protein copies of an antigen's molecular badge are made by injecting nucleic acid (genetic material) from that antigen into a culture of "friendly" bacteria. Friendly bacteria, like the bacteria that live in your stomach to help you digest food, don't harm humans.

When the nucleic acid displaying the antigen's molecular badge is injected into the bacteria, they produce a protein with a molecular badge just like that of the antigen. Scientists can then remove the specific molecular antigen marker from the protein, isolating it. This makes the vaccine safer.

Another approach relies on **anti-antibodies.** Anti-antibodies are part of the immune system's control system. When the commanding generals, your helper T cells and suppressor T cells, call out B cells, the B cells become plasma cells to produce antibodies. These molecular rockets speed to destroy the invader. Just as there is a command system to send antibodies into battle, there is also a command system to call a cease-fire when their work is done. That is the role of the anti-antibody.

An anti-antibody is a protein unit that latches onto the antibody. When the anti-antibody hooks onto the antibody, the antibody stops fighting and destroying. The anti-antibodies declare the battle over and send the antibodies back to the memory fortresses, the lymph nodes, where their immunological memory will remain for a fight another day.

When an anti-antibody is injected as a vaccine, it produces an antibody response without having to use an actual disease-carrying virus. The anti-antibody approach is being studied as a possible vaccine against HIV and cancer. But fighting AIDS or cancer remains a complex and challenging matter.

VACCINES FOR PARASITES

Developing vaccines for parasites presents a more difficult problem than vaccines for viral and bacterial infections. Consider the example of malaria. Malaria is a disease that kills millions of people in tropical areas where malaria-carrying mosquitoes swarm in the jungles. Malaria was a major health problem in the southern regions of the United States until government efforts to kill mosquitoes were successful.

Malaria is caused by a parasite—a protozoan—that enters the body through a mosquito bite. Not all mosquitoes carry this disease, but those that do inject the parasite into the bloodstream. In the bloodstream, the protozoa find red blood cells and enter them. Our immune units do not discover the malaria protozoa because they are hiding in the red blood cells. The parasites kill the red blood cells.

Malaria is treated with medicines such as chloroquine and quinacrine. These medicines work on parasites the same way antibiotics work on bacteria—they compete for food. No vaccine has been found to help the immune system fight malaria, however.

Another parasite that has defied vaccines is the single-celled trypanosome that attacks humans and some animals through the bite of the tsetse fly. The trypanosome keeps changing its appearance by shedding its outer coat. This fools the immune

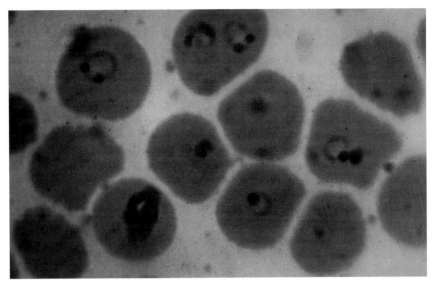

These red blood cells are infected with malarial parasites, seen as dark rings inside the cells.

system into responding as if a new invader has arrived. A new attack is launched—and again, the parasite changes its coat. The process is repeated until the immune system is worn down. Then the trypanosome takes over, and the victim suffers the symptoms of sleeping sickness—drowsiness, laziness, and long periods of inactivity. The victim's nervous system is slowly destroyed, and eventually the person dies.

The need for vaccines for these terrible diseases is obvious and great. Scientists are studying the molecular coats of these parasites, trying to find ways to genetically engineer synthetic vaccines.

Chapter Five

FOOD TO FEED OUR IMMUNE ARMY

"Eat your broccoli—it's good for you."

How many times have you heard that? You know you're supposed to eat your vegetables, especially the ones you don't like. But why? And what does this have to do with your immune system? Good nutrition plays an important role in the prevention of disease. When the body does not get proper nutrients, the immune system slows down and may even turn off.

A well-nourished population is far less likely to suffer epidemic disease than one that is underfed. Centuries ago, great epidemics of cholera, typhus, smallpox, bubonic plague, and scarlet fever took hold as much because of social and dietary conditions as because of the germs that transmit these contagious diseases.

When a Jesuit priest, Father Rucci, traveled through China in the late 1500s, he commented on the amazing good health of the Chinese people. They had energy and vigor up to age 75, while most Europeans were in poor health and died much younger. The difference was diet. But by the early part of the 20th century, Europeans were healthier and living longer, while half of all deaths in China resulted from diet-related diseases.

Colonial Americans ate a broad range of foods, such as game animals, hogs, hominy, cornmeal, peas and beans, molasses,

Starting out the day with a nutritious breakfast is one way to help your immune system.

apples, and bear and other animal oils. They had a naturally balanced diet of simple but sturdy foods. The fast foods so common in the United States 200 years later provide little of the balance needed for good health. Fortunately, many other foods can provide a healthy diet, if we take the time to understand the importance of nutrition.

Good nutrition can enhance the immune systems of individuals as well as larger populations. The foods that help you build a healthy body are the same foods you need to build a healthy immune system. The only problem is that when your body takes in food to feed your hungry organs—such as the brain, the heart, and the lungs—your immune system must wait at the end of the line.

The nutrients you eat are used first to feed your brain and nervous system; next they feed your heart and its blood transportation system. Next in line are your most vital organs— lungs, liver, stomach, kidneys—and after that, your muscles and skin. After they've been cared for, then the white blood cells of the immune system are fed.

THE FUEL OF THE HUMAN ENGINE

When you chew a bite of food, you grind it to a pulp so that you can swallow it. In your stomach, acid reduces the food to a liquid and some fibrous material. This is digestion. The liquid then passes into your small intestine, where the nutrients are absorbed into the walls and passed to the red blood cells for transportation to all the cells of the body. The fibrous food and undigested or unused materials pass into your large intestine and out of your body as waste.

Food is the fuel for your body's operation. The nutrients in food provide the energy to operate all of your body systems. This energy is measured in calories. Scientifically, a calorie is the amount of energy needed to heat 1 gram of water 1 degree Centigrade. (When most people talk about calories, they are referring to a kilocalorie, or 1000 calories, enough energy to heat 100,000 grams [1 kilogram] of water 1 degree Centigrade.)

Your body needs a certain number of calories each day to operate its basic systems. Calories are also needed for mental and physical activity and for growing and repairing damaged or injured body parts. A growing teenager active in school and sports needs far more calories than his or her grandparents, especially if the grandparents spend a lot of time on the recliner in front of the TV.

When the food you eat provides more calories than your body uses, then the excess energy supply is stored as fat, and you gain weight. Of course, the opposite is also true. When you burn more calories than you take in, then you lose weight. Ideally, you should take in only the number of calories that you burn. This balance is not easy to maintain. But there is more to nutrition than calories.

Hand-in-glove with calories are the nutrients: proteins, carbohydrates, fats, vitamins, minerals, and water. You have to balance calories and nutrients when planning a healthy diet. Some foods are very high in calories and low in nutrients. And guess what? These are the foods you love to eat most, like candy and potato chips. An unbalanced diet high in calories and low in important nutrients can affect your immune protection. Other foods, such as lean meats, poultry and fish, peas and beans, whole grains, fruits, and vegetables, are all relatively low in calories and rich in nutrients. These foods provide the mainstay of a balanced diet.

A balanced, healthy diet includes vegetables, fruits, grains, lean meats, fish, and dairy foods.

Packaged and processed foods are usually labeled with the number of calories they contain, along with a list of their nutrients. Many books and magazines provide a great deal of information about calories and nutrients for a wide range of foods.

PROTEINS—THE KEY OF LIFE

You have to have proteins. These extremely complex molecules are a major part of every living cell. In your immune system, protein molecules form your antibodies and the structure of all the white blood cells. They make up your **hormones** and enzymes, which regulate your body functions.

When you lack proteins in your diet, your immune system cannot function. Viruses, bacteria, and parasites find you an easy victim. Sadly, almost one-third of the people in the world do not get enough protein-supplying food.

In the United States, too little protein is seldom a problem; a more common problem is too much of the wrong kind of protein. Excess protein is often stored in the body as fat and can cause damage to the kidneys. Eating too many of certain kinds of proteins can also cause brittle bones and dental problems.

Your brain and glands regulate which parts of your body get the proteins you eat and in what order. Your body has a set of priorities. Your immune system gets last crack at the proteins—it always travels as caboose. If the immune system is at the back of the line when the proteins are passed out, then it's easy to see how a shortage of protein can lead to a lowering of immune protection. During sleep, however, while all of your other body systems are resting in low gear, your immune system gets to work. It grabs incoming proteins and strikes hard at body invaders. That's why you can sometimes go to bed feeling sick and wake up feeling better. Your immune system is doing its job.

WHAT DO PROTEINS LOOK LIKE?

A protein molecule is made up of carbon, hydrogen, oxygen, and nitrogen. You probably know that two atoms of hydrogen and one atom of oxygen together form a simple molecule, water. Carbon, hydrogen, oxygen, and nitrogen can come together as an organic compound called an **amino acid.**

Think of one amino acid molecule as a round bead—a "pop bead" that can be linked with other beads (other amino acid molecules). If we put some of these beads together, we would have a **peptide.** If we linked peptides together in a long chain, we would have a **polypeptide.** Then, if we folded and twisted the polypeptide chain so that it corkscrewed and piled together, we would have a protein molecule.

The sequence in which the beads are put together determines the kind of protein molecule. For example, if each bead were a different color, such as red, blue, green, or yellow, then the order of their arrangement would be important. A protein molecule needed for a certain antibody would have to follow a certain order, such as red, red, yellow, blue, green, green, red, and so forth. The way the string of beads is twisted and piled

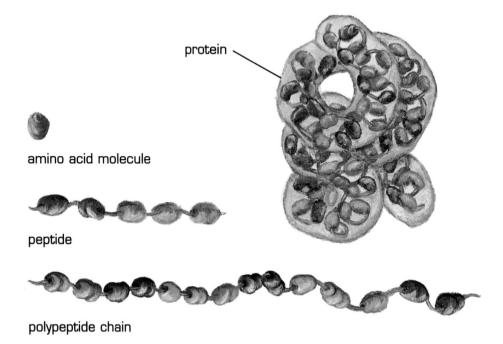

protein

amino acid molecule

peptide

polypeptide chain

determines the nature and type of protein. If it were assembled in a different combination, or twisted and piled in a different way, it would not be an antibody. Of course, the actual amino acid molecules are not color coded like beads, but they are each molecularly different. The order in which amino acids are assembled into polypeptides, and how the protein is twisted and folded, affect the way it does its job.

When the food in your digestive system is dissolved and the proteins are separated and passed along to individual cells, each protein molecule is popped apart into its amino acid components. After these "beads" pass into a cell, they are reassembled as new protein molecules, according to the needs of that cell. We must have the right kinds of amino acids to stay healthy.

There are 22 types of amino acids. Of these 22 types, 13 can be manufactured within your body, while 9 must be supplied by the food you eat. These nine are called essential amino acids. Of the nine essential amino acids, phenylalanine, tryptophan, and valine are necessary to produce antibodies.

Using the bead example, think of the 22 amino acids found in protein as all different colors. Imagine that one of your cells is assembling a protein chain to help it perform the cell's job. To complete the chain, it needs a red bead—one of the essential amino acids. If you never eat any proteins that include red beads—that amino acid—you will have the beginnings of a deficiency problem. Your immune system may not have all the parts necessary to operate as it should.

What should you eat to get the necessary proteins? Proteins are found in many vegetables, nuts, legumes, grains, seeds, and dairy foods, as well as in meats and fish. Only meats and fish contain all the essential amino acids. You can get a full set of essential amino acids without eating either meat or fish, as long

The Amino Acids

The essential amino acids are those you get only from food.
Nonessential amino acids are made by your body.

ESSENTIAL	NONESSENTIAL
Histidine	Alanine
Isoleucine	Arginine
Leucine	Asparagine
Lysine	Aspartine
Methionine	Cysteine
Ornthithine	Cystine
Phenylalanine	Glutamate
Threonine	Glutamine
Tryptophan	Glycine
Valine	Proline
	Serine
	Tyrosine

as you combine non-meat foods so that one food supplies the amino acids missing in another. For example, a meal of rice and kidney beans, or rice with peanuts or black-eyed peas, provides a complete set of essential proteins, because rice contains the amino acids missing in beans, peas, and nuts. Peanut butter on whole wheat bread is another complete protein combination. The same is true of rice and bean curd (tofu), or beans or peas with any of the following: nuts, seeds, grains, cheese, yogurt, or milk.

CARBOHYDRATES—THE MAJOR FUEL

Carbohydrates are your body's primary fuel—your body's energy source. Since carbohydrates provide most of the power for all your body's functions, if you do not get enough carbohydrates in your diet, then your body takes proteins from your immune system to substitute for the carbohydrate loss. This results in a lowering of immune protection.

A carbohydrate molecule is made up of carbon, oxygen, and hydrogen. These molecules range in size and complexity from small and simple to large and complex. The primary source of carbohydrates is plants.

When carbohydrate molecules enter your body, enzymes take a chemical and electrical sledgehammer to them to break them into smaller pieces. This chemical reaction releases energy. The energy, measured in calories, powers your body functions. The amount of energy released is determined by the number of atoms joined together in the carbohydrate molecules. The more complex the molecule, the longer the enzymes take to break it down. The energy from a complex molecule lasts longer than the energy from a simple molecule.

Grains and beans provide important nutrients.

Sugars, starches, and cellulose are different types of carbohydrates. Sugars are the simplest carbohydrate molecules, and, therefore, are burned up quickly by your body. Sugars, like candy bars, are a quick energy source. Starches, such as spaghetti and potatoes, are complex carbohydrates that provide sustained energy. Cellulose is fiber. The carbohydrate molecules of cellulose do not dissolve during digestion. Instead, they pass through the intestines like a great cleansing brush, removing undigested and unused foods from your body. This keeps your body clean and prevents too many bacteria from building up in your intestines.

If you make a point of eating whole grain breads, cereals, and legumes rather than refined starches such as white bread and cereals and pastas made with white flour, you'll be getting cellulose along with the other two types of carbohydrates. Cellulose is also found in most fruits and vegetables.

FATS

Fats are needed to make the membranes (walls) of all cells, including the white blood cells of your immune system. Also, fats, like carbohydrates, provide energy. When fats burn along with carbohydrates, they increase your energy output. Fats store energy so that when your body needs it, it's there.

Without fats, you would have to eat enough carbohydrates each day to supply the whole day's energy needs. On the days when you were short on your carbohydrates, your body would take the carbon, hydrogen, and oxygen from your proteins for energy. This would weaken your immune system and could also cause kidney disease.

Fats are needed in your body to absorb and transport the fat-soluble vitamins—A, D, E, and K. (Fat-soluble vitamins dissolve in fat.) As you probably know, fats make foods taste better—ice cream, whipped cream, juicy hamburgers. Fats also quiet hunger pains by stimulating a hormone that communicates the "all full" message to your brain.

Everybody worries about fat in their diet, but you have to have fat. Fats provide a nice cushion for your body. Every one of your cells is set in fat, like bricks in mortar. A layer of cells stuffed with fat provides insulation just below your skin.

Fat molecules contain the same three elements as carbohydrates—carbon, hydrogen, and oxygen—but in different proportions and arranged differently. The number of hydrogen atoms that combine with the carbon atoms determines whether the fat molecule is *saturated* or *unsaturated*. The more hydrogen, the more saturated the fat. The different chemical nature of saturated and unsaturated fat molecules makes them behave differently.

You can see the difference between saturated and unsaturated fats. At room temperature, saturated fats, such as butter, are firmer, more solid, than unsaturated fats, such as vegetable oil. Unsaturated fats are softer or liquid. This difference affects how your body digests the fat.

The unsaturated, liquid form of fat is more easily digested, while the more solid form is difficult to digest. Much unsaturated fat is stored in the body, producing cholesterol, a chemical that is essential in cells. Most people think of cholesterol as bad. But in the correct proportions, it is essential to good health. Cholesterol is a building block of cell membranes, myelin (the fatty insulation for all your nerve fibers), natural steroid hormones, and bile (a liquid that helps with digestion). In short, eating the right amount of fats, particularly unsaturated fats, along with carbohydrates and proteins, is important to maintain peak health.

On the other hand, too much fat, particularly saturated fat, can lead to trouble with a clogging of arteries and heart disease. Fats from animal foods, such as butter or the fat on meat, are mostly saturated fats, while fats from plant sources, such as corn or olive oil, are usually unsaturated.

VITAMINS AND MINERALS

We cannot complete our understanding of nutrients without discussing vitamins and minerals. A vitamin is a chemical that your body uses as a catalyst. A catalyst is a chemical that helps

Fresh fruits and vegetables are full of vitamins and minerals.

other chemicals combine without itself changing or being involved in the resulting chemical combination. A lack of vitamins can lead to many different diseases.

In your body, vitamins help other nutrients—proteins, carbohydrates, and fats—do their jobs. Some vitamins break down the various elements of the nutrients so they can be reassembled in different forms. Vitamin D is different because it also acts as a chemical messenger, just as hormones do.

There are 13 life-essential vitamins. These divide into two important groups—fat-soluble and water-soluble. When you eat more water-soluble vitamins than you need, they are simply washed out of your body as waste. On the other hand, the fat-soluble vitamins can be dissolved only in hydrogen-rich fats. These vitamins are stored in your body fat. If you take in more of these vitamins than you need, you could have serious health problems. A balanced diet normally gives you all the vitamins necessary to keep your immune system in good working order.

Minerals, like vitamins, are important for helping the basic nutrients work. Minerals control the water and chemical balance in your body. Your immune system always responds to a mineral imbalance, just as it does to a vitamin imbalance. Without the correct mineral intake, B-cell production is short-changed, reducing the number of rockets available for battle.

Minerals are divided into two types, macrominerals and microminerals. The macros are the ones the body needs most—calcium, sodium, chloride, potassium, magnesium, and sulfur. The micros are called trace minerals—iron, zinc, selenium, iodine, copper, chromium, manganese, molybdenum, and fluoride. Of these, zinc appears to be the most important for the immune system. This does not mean that you should try to boost your immune protection by taking a zinc supplement. As with many things, too much can be as harmful as too little. The best way to get the necessary zinc is by eating right. Whole grains, lean meats, eggs, legumes, liver, and seafood are good sources of zinc.

SALT AND WATER

As a machine, your body is fueled by all the nutrients we have just discussed. These nutrients are measured by the calories of energy they produce. Calories produce the electrical energy that operates the whole body. Humans operate by means of tiny electrical charges. Salt and water make these electrical charges happen.

Salt is the compound that results when atoms of sodium and chlorine combine. Sodium and chlorine are both highly active chemical elements. In a water solution with small amounts of

Please Pass the Salt

In medieval times, when the lord of the castle and his attendants gathered for meals at the great table, people of high rank sat "above the salt," while those of lesser station sat "below the salt." Social position was indicated with salt.

As far back as historians can find records, salt has been regarded as a measure of wealth as well as health. Salt was traded as a commodity, and in some instances was considered as valuable as gold. Among the ancient Hebrews, it was the custom to rub salt on a newborn baby as a guarantee of good health.

Roman soldiers received part of their pay in salt, their *salarium*—the Latin origin of the word "salary." In many Middle Eastern countries, salt is a symbol of friendship.

As a food, salt in proper quantities is essential to good health and a properly functioning immune system. But overuse of salt can lead to dangerous health problems.

potassium present, salt separates into sodium and chlorine ions, or charged atoms. The sodium ion is positive and the chlorine ion is negative. These charged particles in the water solution are called electrolytes, a solution through which electrical current can flow.

Normally, if you eat a balanced diet and drink plenty of water, you will get enough salt and water. If you exercise vigorously, then you must drink more water to make up for water loss from sweating. Muscle twinges and cramps are early warnings that your body is out of the proper salt-to-water balance.

Six Rules for Eating Right

1. Keep your intake of fats low. Fats should make up no more than 30 percent of your daily calories. Fats taste good and satisfy hunger, but they do a lot more. High fat intake has been linked to increased cancer risk, to high cholesterol counts, which can lead to arteriosclerosis and heart disease, and to obesity.

2. Eat generous amounts of vegetables and fruit, especially those that are high in vitamins A and C. Most fresh vegetables and fruits are low in fat and high in fiber, vitamins, and minerals. Fruits and vegetables help your body fortify itself against infections and diseases.

3. Eat foods high in fiber. You should be getting 30 to 40 grams of fiber each day; most of us get around 20 grams. Fiber-rich foods like fresh fruits and vegetables, whole grains and cereals, bran, and beans appear to counteract some of the bad effects that fat can have on your health. Dietary fiber fills you up without filling you out.

4. Make your calories count. Eat fewer refined carbohydrates, like white bread, pastries, and refined pastas, grains, and cereals. Instead, eat more complex carbohydrates, such as whole wheat bread, whole grains and cereals, peas, and beans. You'll cut down on calories and eat more fiber. Because complex carbohydrates burn slowly, they give you long-lasting energy.

5. Pay particular attention to what you eat during times of stress, when your body is pulling reserves from your immune system to feed other body systems.

6. Eat a substantial breakfast, as well as a good lunch and dinner. Make breakfast the most important meal of the day and include some low-fat protein and complex carbohydrates in it. Don't skimp on lunch or dinner, either. We're not talking about calories here, but nutrients.

This is followed by fatigue and lowered immune protection.

You can survive for long periods of time without food, but for only a few days without water. A prolonged period without water leads to serious problems. Blood movement slows down, lymph fluid thickens, and the immune system loses its main rivers for transportation. As a result, your body is more susceptible to an invasion by bacteria, viruses, or parasites. Water also regulates body temperature, cooling the body by evaporation as we sweat.

When the body loses water, the salt content goes up. A loss of water (called dehydration) is not the same as perspiration, which removes both salt and water. Increased salt in the body can cause cell death. When cells die, they cannot be replaced. Dehydration can lead to death.

Chapter Six

THE MIND-BODY CONNECTION

Over the centuries, healers of all sorts have used spells and rituals to convince people who were sick that they had the power to get well. Tribal medicine men achieved positions of power because they were successful in curing their patients.

Even though their knowledge of medicine was limited, these healers relied on an important key to health: the mind-body connection. What was, and still is, important is that the patients believed the doctor would make them well. Faith in the healer is what counts. There is a powerful connection between what you think and your health.

Your immune system functions by a series of commands from your brain. Electrical impulses flash along your nerves, and hormone and protein messengers carry chemical instructions to your immune system. Your immune system talks back, sending its messages to your brain via chemicals called **cytokines.** With this exchange of information and commands, your immune system tends to its job. If your brain commands it, your immune system activities can be increased—more white blood cells can be produced to attack an invading microorganism. It's as if your brain is an amplifier for your immunological CD player.

So when a tribal doctor treated a patient with a ritual, the patient believed he would be cured. His brain sent a message to

Exercise and sports can help you deal with stress, which in turn is good for your immune system.

[71]

his immune system to increase production of disease-fighting white blood cells, which helped him get well. Although people have relied on "magic" healing for over 5,000 years, it has only been in the last few decades that medical scientists have been able to demonstrate that you can turn your immune system on or off by how you think.

This idea was first demonstrated in the laboratory in 1975 by a psychologist, Dr. Robert Ader, and an immunologist, Dr. Nicholas Cohen, at the University of Rochester in New York. They gave rats an experimental drug to slow down their immune systems. To get the rats to drink the medicine, they sweetened it with saccharine water. The rats drank it eagerly. When the rats took the medicine with the sweetened water, their immune systems shut down. The medicine worked. But when the doctors gave the same rats plain sweetened water, without the medicine, their immune systems shut down just the same as if they were getting the drug.

This experiment resembled the work by Ivan Pavlov, the Russian physiologist who won a Nobel Prize in 1904 when he proved that the mind could affect the body's responses. Pavlov trained his dog to understand that whenever he rang a bell, the dog's food would be served. Normally, the dog would salivate whenever he saw his food. Over time, the dog learned to connect the ringing of the bell with eating. Soon the dog was salivating whenever the bell was rung, without any food before him. Pavlov called this a conditioned reflex, and it was the first proof of the mind-body connection.

We have since learned that the mind communicates with the immune system, issuing electrical and chemical commands, while the immune system sends messages back chemically. And, like the brain, the immune system has memory. When the immune system "remembers" that it met an invader before, it searches through its inventory of antibody-producing B cells in the lymph nodes and rushes the correct antibodies to attack the invader. Only our brains and our immune systems have memory.

If, on the other hand, a bacteria or virus invades your body for the first time, it can take many days for the immune system to process the information, develop the necessary antibodies, and manufacture enough of them to destroy the invader. You may be sick for a number of days before you begin to recover. During part of the time you're sick, you might have a fever. When your immune system sends an urgent message to the brain that it needs help until all its artillery can be put in place, your **hypothalamus**—the part of your brain that controls body temperature, among other things—increases your body temperature. This increase in body temperature—the fever—helps to kill germs.

YOUR ATTITUDE COUNTS

If you are a happy, upbeat person, convinced of your good health and your ability to overcome any disease that comes along, then you can help your immune system. By facing challenges with a winner's spirit, you can affect your body's immune regulation. A smile and an optimistic attitude will signal your immune system to produce more white blood cells.

On the other hand, if you are upset, anxious, or fearful, you can unknowingly cause your immune system to slow down, making it easier for an invading germ to make you sick.

Try this exercise. Close your eyes and take a deep breath. Relax your entire body. Now focus your attention on an imaginary screen. You see a virus—the enemy—climbing down the back of your throat. Maybe you see it as blood-red checkers on a checkerboard—the checkerboard is your throat. Next you see the forces of good—the black checkers on the other side of your throat. You direct the black checkers to jump the red checkers and remove them from the board. You win the checker game.

Now the checkers dissolve in your mind and become moving Pac-Man–shaped players. Just as if you were playing a video game, you envision your Pac-Men gobbling up viruses. You do this over and over. You force all other thoughts from your mind and focus your attention on these images. You are trying to help your white blood cells fight infection.

This game is not a game at all. It is a developing science known as **psychoneuroimmunology.** Dr. Steven Locke of Harvard University and Dr. Bernie Siegel of Yale University were early promoters of this science. Combining conventional cancer therapy with guided imagery, Dr. Locke achieved remarkable results. Guided imagery is like the exercise you just did—a way to imagine something you want to happen. A number of scientists are researching the psychological effects of different diseases on the immune system. The National Institutes of Health is looking into mental imagery as an "alternative" medicine.

Imagery does not work for everyone. It requires intense concentration, much like meditation. While many people meditate, others cannot master the technique.

STRESS

A certain amount of stress is a natural and expected part of life. Do you recall the first time you had to go up on stage in front of a crowd of people to act or sing? Remember that hard knot in your stomach, or feeling a little sick, or how your palms were sweaty? Those were signs of stress—the stress that prepares your body for action.

The human body is designed for this stressful intensity. It is often referred to as the "fight or flight" response. Stress is nature's way of organizing your nerves, muscles, blood, and organs into a protective mode. As you face a stressful or dangerous situation, your blood pressure goes up and your heart speeds up. Your digestive tract shuts down and you may feel a little queasy. You feel a boost of energy as your body's chemistry turns proteins into glucose (a type of sugar) for quick energy.

It all begins in the brain. When you perceive a stressful situation (through your senses—sight, hearing, feeling, and so on), these perceptions are conveyed to the hypothalamus. The hypothalamus sends hormone messengers to your **pituitary gland,** which lies at the base of your brain. The pituitary gland, in turn, sends hormone messengers to other glands, which signal your organs and muscles to prepare for action. One of the glands that receives these instructions is your adrenal gland. The adrenal gland pumps out **adrenaline** and **steroids** as part of the fight or flight response. Adrenaline raises blood pressure, and the steroids shut down immune activity to direct all the energy to fighting or fleeing.

So your body parts are "pumped up," except the immune system. It slows down, leaving your body with a lowered resistance to disease and infection. For short periods, there's no harm done; your body adapts easily. But if you go through a severely stressful situation, or it lasts a long time, or such situations happen frequently, your health can be jeopardized. This is known as *distress*.

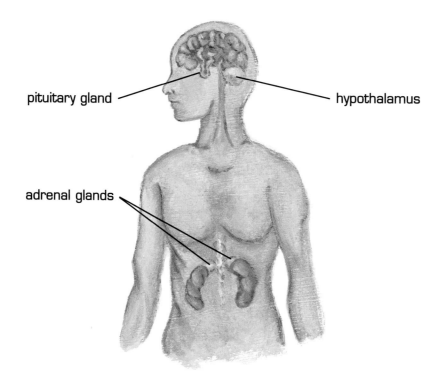

pituitary gland

hypothalamus

adrenal glands

Frustration, anger, fear, anxiety, or depression can lower your body's resistance to disease. A patient who reacts with shock and depression when confronted with the sudden news that she has a cancerous tumor might shut down her own immune system and speed the growth of the cancer. Another patient faced with the same news who reacts by saying "I can beat this disease" can help her immune system.

One medical study showed that college students undergoing the normal stresses of final examinations were more susceptible to colds, flu, and other infections during examinations.

SUDDEN OR EXTREME COLD

Stress to your immune system can come from several sources. One source is cold. As warm-blooded animals, humans are designed to have a relatively constant body temperature. If you dash outside on a cold day without a coat, your body is immediately stressed. Adrenaline (also called **epinephrine**) is released and your body chemistry changes. If you sit in a cold, drenching rain for a long time, the stress becomes *distress,* and those hormone messengers fly into high gear. Your thyroid slows down, processing fewer white blood cells. Your adrenal gland produces more hormones and increases blood pressure for more body heat. You are ready to battle the cold temperature, but there are fewer T cells, B cells, and antibodies to fight viruses or bacteria. If, unknown to you, your immune system had been quietly fighting off a bacterial or viral infection and you stayed very cold for a long time, your immune system might shut down long enough to allow the germs to escape the soldiers of your system.

While getting cold will not in itself give you a cold, it can make you more likely to catch one. That's why your mother says, "Bundle up, you don't want to catch a cold."

PAIN

Pain is the way the brain interprets messages from nerves that an injury, disorder, or disease is taking place. When the brain receives these messages, it issues commands. These commands instruct your nerves to direct an instant reaction. For example, you pull your hand back from a hot stove or blink your eye when a gnat invades. You react to stop the pain. The nerves may also direct some involuntary changes, such as increased heart rate and faster breathing.

Pain also creates stress and puts you into the fight-or-flight mode. If pain is prolonged or constant, as with such diseases as arthritis, cancer, and liver or kidney disorders, then the stress of pain becomes distress and the slowed immune system increases the risk for other diseases. Depression triggered by chronic pain also increases the likelihood of disease.

GET SOME SLEEP

"All you need is a good night's sleep." That's good advice, but nobody told you exactly why.

Sleep is the body's repair shop. When you sleep, your body resets all its stress clocks. Your body systems slow down during sleep—except your immune system. Remember that when the proteins are passed out, your immune system is at the back of the line? Not when you sleep. While all the other body systems slow down—major organs are at rest, heartbeat is slower, and breathing more relaxed—your immune system is first in line for proteins, vitamins, and minerals. The amino acids are made available for the production of antibodies. During the first few hours of deep sleep, your pituitary gland sends out hormone messengers to deliver the protein supply where it's needed to produce white blood cells.

Often, sleep is the best prescription for fighting infection. It is not by accident that you can wake up cured of an illness. On the other hand, a lack of sleep, or even disturbed sleep, can slow recovery or make you more susceptible to a disease.

Sleep occurs in stages. One important stage is called REM sleep, which stands for *rapid eye movement;* another is called NREM or deep sleep, standing for *non-rapid eye movement.*

Getting a good night's sleep is like taking your body to a repair shop.

REM sleep is characterized by dreams and a flickering of the eyes back and forth under closed eyelids. NREM is a deeper, quieter sleep. Your blood pressure drops, your heart rate slows down, your breathing becomes slower and more even, and your body temperature falls. During the night, you pass in and out of these stages several times.

Each stage of sleep has its own functions. Experiments have demonstrated that not getting one or the other type can have serious consequences. In REM sleep, your body is resting, but your brain remains fully active. This is the period of active dreaming. Dreaming is not completely understood, but some scientists believe that dreaming is the way your brain sorts out sights, sounds, emotions, and thoughts from the day and organizes what is to be kept in your memory, where it will be stored, and what should be discarded or forgotten.

In NREM sleep, all energy requirements are lowered. The immune system functions at its highest level, sweeping the body of invading germs. In experiments where volunteers were allowed only REM sleep and not NREM sleep, the volunteers became sluggish and depressed. If people do not get NREM sleep for a prolonged period, they can suffer severe psychological damage. Lack of REM sleep leads to irritability and disorientation. You need both REM and NREM sleep to stay healthy.

HANDLING STRESS

It is not possible to live without stress. A certain amount of stress is healthy, and the line between what is healthy and what is unhealthy is fuzzy. But there are ways to deal with stress that can be helpful to you and your immune system. Here are seven rules for handling stress:

1. *Eat properly.* Under stress, some people gorge on junk food or don't eat at all. When you're under stress, eating a balanced, nutritional diet is extra important. Prolonged stress dumps hormones into your bloodstream, and enzymes use much of your protein intake and destroy vitamins and minerals. A well-balanced diet can do much to offset the negative effects of stress. If you are under a lot of stress, such as when you have a big test coming up, help your body by eating well.

2. *Get enough sleep.* Remember what we have just described about the importance of sleep.

3. *Confide your problems to a parent, other family member, or friend.* Being able to talk to a caring person about your problems is important for good mental and physical health.

4. *Express your feelings with words.* Writing in a journal about problems has long been recognized as an effective tool for releasing tension.

5. *Relax for at least 30 minutes a day.* Different people have different ways to relax—walking, hobbies such as models or painting, meditation, listening to music, reading a book, playing a video game. Relaxation helps reduce stress.

6. *Exercise.* Some form of exercise is important to everyone. Physical exercise helps to maintain muscle tone, increase blood circulation, and exercise your heart muscle. For the immune system, exercise counteracts the negative effects of stress.

7. *Avoid alcohol and drugs.* While alcohol or drugs might temporarily numb your mind and seem like a good way to handle stress, your immune system, already slowed down by distress, will shut down further from alcohol or drugs.

Chapter Seven

ALLERGIES—WHEN THE IMMUNE SYSTEM REACTS

Two out of every ten people suffer from some form of **allergy,** a disorder that arises from a hyperactive immune system. This condition is known as **hypersensitivity.** People who are not hypersensitive can breathe, taste, and touch things that are a normal part of the environment without suffering. The unlucky 20 percent of people who are hypersensitive have immune systems that overreact to one or more things. Their immune systems are too vigorous in defending against certain foreign invaders.

For people with allergies, a bee sting or a shot of penicillin can cause more than a brief pain. An allergic reaction can cause red, itching hives, or worse—wheezing and gasping for air as the bronchial tubes begin to swell shut.

In the spring, as you inhale the sweet perfume of flowering honeysuckle, you may also breathe in the invisible pollen from the sycamore tree. If you are allergic to that pollen, you might start sneezing, your eyes might water, and your nose might run.

A glass of milk, a piece of cheese, a sesame-seed roll, pollen, dust, feathers, and dander (flakes of dried skin) from a dog or cat can all trigger an allergic reaction. Almost anything can cause an allergic reaction. But some things are more likely to be *allergenic*—to cause allergies—than others.

The pollen grains from cattails and other plants can trigger allergic reactions in some people.

The particles that cause hypersensitive reactions are special antigens called **allergens.** If we are hypersensitive, our immune system responds to those particles by producing a special, potent series of antibodies. An allergic reaction can be immediate or delayed, occurring hours or even days after exposure to the allergen. For instance, a bee sting can cause a violent allergic reaction almost immediately, while an allergic reaction to poison ivy may not appear until two or three days later.

Hay fever, a common allergy that causes watery eyes and a runny nose, has nothing to do with hay. The villains are microscopic pollen grains from numerous trees, weeds, and grasses in

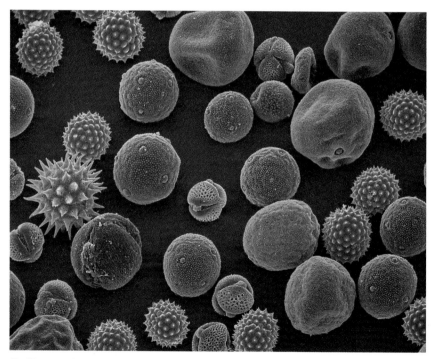

Pollen grains come in many shapes and sizes.

their pollinating stage. Because the start of the pollinating stage coincides with the springtime mowing of hay, the allergy was called "hay fever."

Some allergies change over time. If you are an allergy sufferer, you may grow out of your allergies. Unfortunately, you may also develop new ones.

Some children and adults are allergic to cow's milk. (Many other people can't drink milk because of lactose intolerance, caused by the absence of a certain enzyme.) The connection between drinking milk and stomach pains and diarrhea has been observed for over 200 years. Children have a greater chance of developing an allergy to cow's milk if they are bottle-fed rather than breast-fed. This is true for children of nonallergic parents as well as children of allergic parents. A mother's milk provides a source of immunity for the baby, protecting her baby's developing intestines from the foreign protein in cow's milk until the infant's own immune system develops.

How Allergies Work

People who suffer from allergies are described as allergic or hypersensitive. If you are not hypersensitive, any allergens you breathe in are met in the moist tissues of your throat, bronchial tubes, or lungs by the first line of defense, the macrophages. These white blood cells, along with certain other types of white blood cells, encircle and destroy the invading microorganisms, and you never even realize you sucked up an allergen.

When an allergen enters your body, the T-cell committee of helper cells and suppressor cells signals the alarm to the B cells to begin production of antibodies. These antibodies are called **Immunoglobulin E,** or IgE. They act as a patrol, circulating in the blood and lymph system and looking for entering allergens. When they find them, they carry the allergens to special cells.

Some of these special cells, like battle stations, have a permanent home base in the skin, while others roam the universe of your body. The permanent battle stations are called **mast cells,** and the floating ones are called **basophils.** Whenever an IgE antibody seizes an invader, it carries the invader to the nearest battle station—a mast cell or basophil. The mast cell or the basophil releases a small puff of chemicals, mostly histamine, as it engulfs and destroys the allergen.

In a hypersensitive person, an allergen causes these commands to become confused. The helper T cells and suppressor T cells do not receive a clear signal, and they do not command the B cells to stop making IgE antibodies. Ten times the number of antibodies than are needed for the task are produced. They quickly overload the mast cells and basophils, which release large amounts of histamines and histaminelike substances. The release of large doses of histamines can produce watery eyes, runny nose, itching, wheezing, sneezing, and even vomiting or stomachaches—all symptoms of an allergic reaction. Antihistamines are given to counteract an allergic reaction by chemically blocking the ability of histamines to do their work.

The same thing happens with food allergies. Food allergens enter the bloodstream through the walls of the small intestine, where they are met by the roving IgE antibodies. The antibodies carry the allergens to the mast cells and basophils. The same kind of explosion of histamine and histaminelike chemicals occurs. Again, the results are an allergic reaction.

You can picture the basophil as a Velcro-covered ball that collects delicate Y-shaped particles on its surface. Each particle or small group of particles—the IgE antibodies—has collected

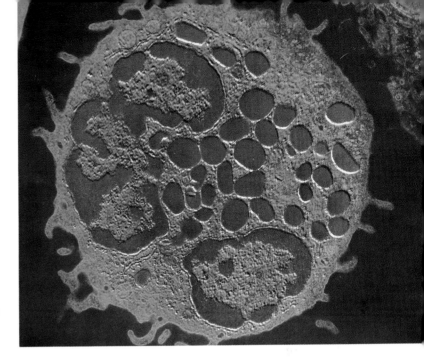

The red granules inside this basophil are packed with histamine and other chemicals. The cell's nucleus is shown in red and green.

any allergens it passes, bringing them to the cell. Each particle sets off a release of histamine. Thousands of these IgE antibodies flock to the cell, and it is overloaded. Unfortunately, if you have one allergy, you may have a second one or even more. Mast cells can become overloaded with antibodies responding to more than one type of allergen.

If you are allergic to cats and have been around a cat, you may have begun to load the mast cells. But if they are not yet overloaded, you have not had an allergic reaction. If you are also allergic to cheese, then eating just a small bite of cheese could tip the scales. The mast cells become overloaded, triggering an allergic reaction.

An allergic reaction to a food can occur no matter what form the food takes. If you are allergic to eggs, then you may have a reaction when you eat any food made with eggs—cakes, cookies, quiche, egg noodles. If your allergy is to corn, then cornmeal, corn starch, corn syrup, and corn oil can all cause a reaction.

Allergies to food are often hard to identify because of the complexities of diet and the mixtures of foods involved. For example, someone who is highly allergic to eggs could be very careful not to eat omelets, but if that person ate a cookie, not knowing that it was made with eggs, he or she could suffer a serious allergic reaction.

Your physical condition can also affect an allergic reaction. If you are cold, upset, or ill, you may be more susceptible to an antibody overload or a hypersensitive reaction. The signals to your brain override the normal immune commanders.

PREVENTING ALLERGIES

The best way to protect yourself from an allergic reaction is to know what you are allergic to and avoid the allergen whenever possible. If your allergy is to certain grasses or trees, then pay attention to the cycle of pollination where you live. Staying in an air-conditioned building will help. In your home, be sure the air filters are kept clean. An electronic filter incorporated in a central heating and air-conditioning system will help.

If your allergy is to mold or fungi, be aware that they can be especially heavy around grains, trees, and other plants in the country. Summer cottages that have been closed for the winter can be full of mold.

If your allergy is to dust, you are probably allergic to dust mites. These multilegged creatures shaped like wood ticks are so small they can ride the air on particles of dust and you cannot see them. Actually, it is not usually the mites themselves that cause allergic reactions, but the mite droppings. Careful vacuuming, regular cleaning, and good air filters can help relieve the discomfort of a dust allergy.

If your allergy is to certain foods, then you have to watch what you eat. The same is true of drugs and medications. If you are allergic to penicillin, this should be noted in your medical record. You will probably be asked to wear a medical alert necklace or bracelet, because an allergic reaction to penicillin can be fatal. This is also true if you are allergic to bee stings. You should not only wear a medical alert medallion, but you should carry an insect-sting kit if you are on a hike or a picnic where you may be around bees.

TREATMENT FOR ALLERGIES

If you have an allergy, you may be able to get shots to protect you from the discomforts and dangers of allergic reactions. The doctor begins by injecting small amounts of suspected allergens into your skin. If your skin turns red, this tells the doctor that the substance injected is causing an allergic reaction. After identifying the allergen, the doctor gives you a series of small injections of the substance. This begins building an immunity in your system. As these small amounts of allergen are injected, the helper T cells and the suppressor T cells receive the information that your body has been invaded by a foreign protein. The first, early antibodies made by your B cells are **Immunoglobulin-G** (IgG). IgG antibodies do not react with allergens in the same way as IgE—they do not cause the release of histamine. Since they compete with IgE for the allergen, over time they will be faster to reach the allergen and destroy it. Eventually, the IgE will no longer react. So the next time you encounter the allergen, before the B cells can prepare IgE antibodies, the smaller, faster IgG antibodies will rush in. They will destroy the allergens and prevent IgE antibodies from

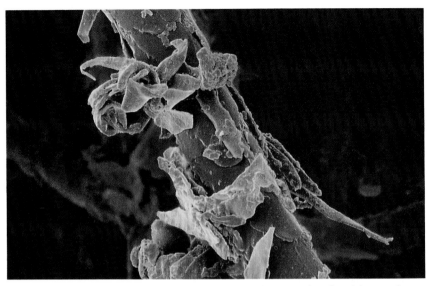

Your dog or cat may be innocent enough, but its dander (shown here on a single hair) is a problem for some hypersensitive people.

reacting with the allergens. Slowly, your immunological memory becomes enlarged.

Many asthma attacks in children are a form of hypersensitive allergic reaction. The allergic reaction to dust, pollen, food, or other substances causes the linings of the lungs to become inflamed and swollen. Some cases of asthma happen because of smaller or constricted airways in the lungs. But when asthma is a result of an allergic reaction, the preventive steps for allergic reactions will ease the suffering.

DELAYED HYPERSENSITIVITY

A delayed allergic reaction results from an entirely different set of immune system reactions than an immediate allergic reaction. **Delayed hypersensitivity** is not caused by overactive IgE antibodies, but by an overstimulation of the T cells. Remember that white blood cells are programmed into various types, such as macrophages, lymphocytes, killer T cells, and leukocytes. All of these are T cells. Delayed hypersensitivity occurs slowly, as its name suggests, usually over many days, sometimes even a week.

The rash caused by poison ivy is a form of delayed hypersensitive reaction. If you are predisposed to hypersensitivity, then when your skin is confronted by the oil on a poison ivy leaf, sensitized T cells rush to that area of the skin to attack the allergen. Not only do they destroy the invader, but they also destroy surrounding cells. As a result, red wheals and raised pink rashes pop out on the surface of your skin. Because it may take the T cells a day or two to process the allergen, the reaction is delayed. You suffer with an itchy rash days after you walked through a patch of poison ivy.

The rejection of a skin graft or an organ transplant is another form of delayed hypersensitivity. You've probably read news stories about organ transplants. Often the doctor reports that the operation was successful, but the doctor and patient are waiting to see if the patient's body will reject the transplanted organ. This means they are waiting for the possibility of a delayed hypersensitive reaction. Tissue typing helps to reduce the likelihood of organ rejection. Cells are studied to determine if there is a good molecular match between the cells of the organ recipient and those of the donor. In addition, medicine that slows down the immune system response helps make organ transplantation successful.

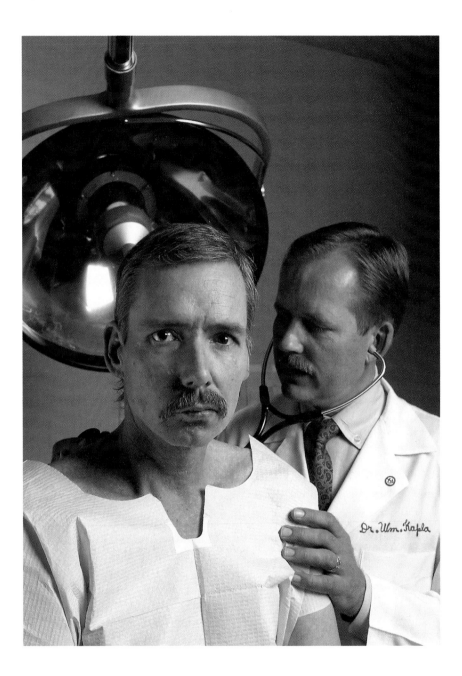

Chapter Eight

WHEN THE IMMUNE SYSTEM FAILS

Is it possible for your immune system to stop working? Or to overwork? Or never to have worked at all? The answer is yes to all three questions. Your immune system can be defective in whole or in part from birth, it can break down, or it can become misdirected and turn against you. When the immune system is defective from birth or breaks down, the disorder is called **immunodeficiency.** When your immune system turns against you, the disorder is called **autoimmunity.**

WHEN THE IMMUNE SYSTEM IS DEFECTIVE

As you have learned, the immune system is the army that protects us from the dangerous environment in which we live. Allergies and other hypersensitive reactions happen when the immunological units aren't working perfectly. But what would happen if your immune system never did work? You would suffer from various diseases, depending on which part of the system did not work.

If your genetic code contains a defect, then you may be born without part or all of your immune system. The most serious immunological defect is a total absence of T cells and B cells. This is called severe combined immunodeficiency disease, or

A patient with AIDS, a disease that destroys the immune system, is examined by his doctor.

SCID. A baby who is born without an immune system, that is, without stem cells to generate white blood cells, lacks any immune protection. The child will be overwhelmed by infections of all sorts and has no chance of survival without medical help.

In 1971, a baby with SCID was born in Houston, Texas. He was known only as David. He was nicknamed "the bubble boy" because he had to live in a totally germ-free enclosure, an isolated "bubble." As long as he stayed in the bubble, he could avoid all forms of body invaders, but out of the bubble, he would likely die from the first infectious germ that came along. As he grew older, NASA built a small space suit for him so he

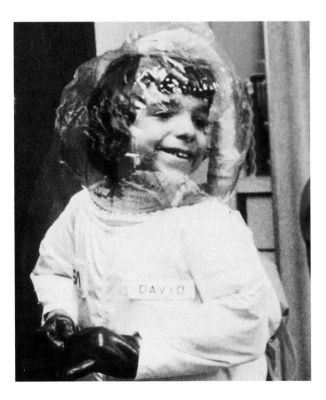

David, the "bubble boy," was able to move around in a space suit that NASA made for him.

could spend time in the backyard with his family. David would never be able to leave his protected enclosure unless he could receive a new immune system through a bone marrow transplant. If his body accepted a bone marrow transplant, new stem cells would begin manufacturing white blood cells and he might have a chance for a normal, healthy life. Some bone marrow transplants have been successful with other SCID patients.

When David was 12 years old, the doctors decided to attempt a transplant of bone marrow from his sister, who had a healthy immune system and was a close immunological match. But an undetectable virus, inactive and hidden in his sister's immune system, passed to David in the transplant. Without immune protection, he was unable to defeat the sudden viral attack, and he soon died.

If a child is born without a thymus or with a malformed thymus, then T cells are not produced. The resulting disease is called DiGeorge syndrome. Again, a bone marrow transplant is the only effective cure for this disorder.

If the defect is the absence of B cells, then no antibodies can be produced. This disorder is called hypogammaglobulin anemia. The disorder is treated by injections of **gamma globulin.** Gamma globulin is the part of the blood that contains antibodies. It provides the patient with a temporary dose of antibodies. With injections every other week, the patient can lead a normal life.

Each immune unit has its own specialized function or functions. If there's a defect of any one or combination of these types, then there is a corresponding disease.

Genetic immunodeficiency includes a long list of approximately 70 disorders, but the three we have discussed—SCID, DiGeorge syndrome, and hypogammaglobulin anemia—are the most common.

Gene therapy is now used by doctors to treat SCID and other immune deficiencies. Bone marrow cells are removed from the patient and a corrected copy of the defective gene in the stem cells is inserted into them. Then the altered marrow cells are put back into the patient. If all goes well, a normal immune system will result.

AIDS

AIDS is another form of immunodeficiency. This disease, however, is not the result of a genetic defect at birth. It is caused by a virus. It leads to the loss of part of the immune system. AIDS stands for acquired immune deficiency syndrome. This means there is a *deficiency* or defect in your immune system, but you *acquired* it—you were not born with it.

A virus called human immunodeficiency virus, or HIV, invades your body, then seeks a manufacturing plant. Remember, viruses cannot reproduce themselves. They need a host. So they attach to a cell, penetrate the cell wall, and enter into the nucleus sea within the cell. In the cell, the virus sheds its molecular coat, empties its own nucleic acid into the host cell, changes the DNA code within the cell, and finally causes the host cell to become a manufacturing plant for more viruses. Ultimately, the host cell dies, but not before billions of new, deadly viruses have been manufactured.

The AIDS virus is especially dangerous because of the host cell it attacks—the helper T cell. The helper T cell is one of the two generals commanding and controlling all the other units of your immune system. As these helper cells are destroyed, all commands become garbled or no commands are even made. No new antibodies are produced, and no killer T cells are produced.

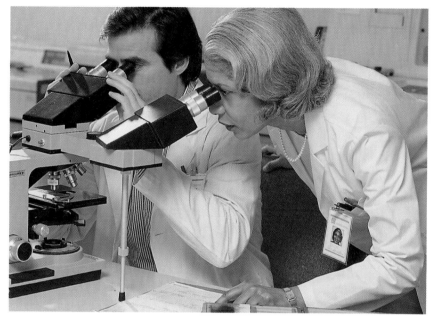

Researchers are searching for a cure or vaccine for AIDS.

In short, no immune work gets done.

A person with AIDS has a reduced immune function; he or she has an immune deficiency. Just like the "bubble boy," people with an immune-deficiency are susceptible to many other diseases—attacks by other viruses, bacteria, parasites, or fungi. Lung infections, pneumonia, mouth infections, and skin cancer are some of the illnesses that people with AIDS may get.

While a bone marrow transplant may work to restore the immune system in cases of SCID, with AIDS, a bone marrow transplant will not work. HIV will infect and eventually kill any new helper T cells.

HIV is very aggressive, reproducing at thousands of times the speed of other viruses. In addition, HIV mutates; that is, it changes its protein markings. When the virus first invades the body, it enters white blood cells. It remains totally inactive for a long time, two to ten years. Many people who are found to have HIV in their blood do not show any sign of the disease AIDS. How long a virus will remain inactive or what causes a dormant virus to become active is unknown. These are questions scientists are pursuing in their search for a cure or a vaccine for AIDS.

Before he died in 1995, Dr. Jonas Salk, the developer of the first polio vaccine, was working on a vaccine that would energize certain killer T cells to pursue HIV and the infected helper T cells. He wanted to destroy not only the virus but the host cells while the virus was inactive. His plan was to develop an artificial way to stimulate the immune system to recognize HIV. This would cause the body's immune units to seek and destroy HIV. This is one of many avenues of research being pursued. Work in gene therapy also provides hope in the search for a cure.

Until a cure is discovered, the best defense against AIDS is prevention and protection. HIV is passed from one person to another by the direct mixing of body fluids. The most common form of transmission is through sexual contact. A second major source of transmission is infection through needles used by intravenous drug users. A third source is the transfusion of blood or blood products from an infected person to an uninfected one. For that reason, AIDS antibody screening tests are required at all blood donor banks. Finally, the virus can also pass from an infected mother to her unborn child.

HIV is delicate and cannot live outside the warmth and shelter of body fluids for more than 15 minutes. This means that the infection cannot be spread by touching, coughing, or sneezing.

WHEN THE BODY ATTACKS ITSELF

Do you remember the three characteristics of the immune system? They are memory, specificity, and distinguishing self from nonself. As white blood cells and antibodies flow throughout your body, they are always searching for foreign invaders, the outsiders. But when your immune army fails to recognize self and begins to attack your own body parts, you have an autoimmune disease.

As we already discussed, before birth every cell is given a molecular badge. Your immune system has all of your millions of parts catalogued. When your system makes a mistake and misreads a molecular badge, it sees a normal, self cell as foreign. A command goes out: There is a foreign invader in our midst! Killer T cells and antibodies then launch an attack on your own body. This attack is an autoimmune reaction.

For instance, in multiple sclerosis and other diseases of the nervous system, the attack takes place within the brain and spinal cord. The immunological army eats holes in the nerve linings, disrupting the flow of signals along the nerves to the muscles and causing paralysis.

Rheumatoid arthritis, systemic lupus erythematosus, and some forms of encephalitis are all autoimmune diseases. Why autoimmune diseases occur is not known for sure. Scientists think it is likely that some cells failed to get logged into the catalog—at birth, these cells were not properly marked with the molecular badge of "self." It's also possible that viral infections could alter some of the badges, making them targets for the immune army. Some alterations of the immune system make enemies of the body's own white blood cells.

Chapter Nine

MEDICINE OF THE FUTURE

As we move into the 21st century, scientists are using their knowledge of the immune system to find new ways to fight disease. The new work is often referred to as the molecular biology revolution, an explosion of knowledge based on detailed cellular and molecular studies of the immune system.

THE MIRROR IMAGE VACCINE PROMISE

Niels Jerne, an **immunologist,** won a Nobel Prize for his pioneering work in developing the theory that anti-antibodies help regulate the immune system. Anti-antibodies are part of the control scheme of the immune system. They stop regular antibodies from continuing to damage cells after all the invaders have been destroyed. Anti-antibodies are like the chaperones who call an end to the party. They turn off the music and tell the antibodies that the party is over and they must go home. The molecular shapes on the receptors of anti-antibodies fit like puzzle pieces with the antibodies' receptor ends—the tops of the two prongs of the "Y."

From this concept, Dr. Henry Kunkel of the Rockefeller Institute is studying a technique to create special mirror-image anti-antibodies to fool the immune system into creating a new

At a molecular biology laboratory, a scientist fills a sample tray with biological samples during DNA research. Genetic and gene therapy are important aspects of cutting-edge immunology.

Immunologist Niels Jerne celebrated after winning the Nobel Prize for medicine in 1984.

set of antibodies to an imaginary antigen. Since the anti-antibody is not an actual microbe but a mirror of the antibody, it will cause no harm to the body. By using anti-antibodies, it is not necessary to use even a small amount of real virus to create a vaccine. It would be dangerous to use a virus such as HIV or Ebola in a vaccine, even if the virus were killed. But a vaccine made from anti-antibodies cannot cause a disease.

MUTANTS

Equally as exciting as anti-antibodies are receptor mutants. If you had fun watching movies or playing video games of the Teenage Mutant Ninja Turtles, then you are ready for receptor mutants. A mutant is an organism that has changed or "mutated." If a person's genes changed or mutated from how they were originally, they are mutant genes.

In the summer of 1996, Stephen O'Brien of the National Cancer Institute, along with Michael Dean and Mary

Carrington, completed a study to show that certain people with a particular mutant cell were resistant to the AIDS virus. These lucky few had a natural immunity to this disease. In the average person, HIV locks onto helper T cells, then enters these cells and destroys them. The AIDS virus is designed to attack only the helper cells. More specifically, the AIDS virus will attack only cells with helper T-cell receptors, like a key fitting into a lock. People with natural immunity do not have ordinary locks on their helper T cells. One of their receptors is a mutant. As a result, the AIDS virus key doesn't fit the lock and cannot enter the cell. This discovery has raised hopes of developing AIDS therapies and vaccines.

ORGANS FROM ANIMALS AND MACHINES

Transplanting kidneys, livers, and hearts from one person to another has become commonplace. But there are far more patients who need replacement organs than there are organs available for them. Many patients die before a suitable replacement organ can be found. Because of this shortage, the use of animal organs for transplantation into humans has been considered. This is called xenotransplantation. Experiments involving this approach to organ transplantation began in the 1960s. The early work was not successful.

In 1984, an infant was born prematurely with a defective heart. Only half of her heart had developed. She was expected to live only a few weeks with this condition. Her parents and physicians decided to make a daring attempt to save the baby's life by transplanting the heart of a baboon into her. (No human heart of the correct size was available.) On October 26 of that year, the operation was performed. The little girl, "Baby Fae," was the first human to be implanted with an animal's heart. Within a few weeks, however, her heart showed signs of a serious immunological attack, and she soon died. The immune system attack was not against the new heart, as expected, but against the blood type of the baboon. Baby Fae had type O blood, while the baboon had AB. Their incompatibility triggered the immune system attacks that caused her death.

Interest in the possibility of using animal organs for transplantation continued. In 1992, Dr. Thomas Starzl of the University of Pittsburgh transplanted a baboon liver into a patient who was in a coma and dying of liver failure. The operation appeared to be successful. Within five days, the man was up and walking. But while his new liver functioned well, he began to suffer from a fungal infection caused by the operation. This infection was followed by a fatal brain hemorrhage.

The operation, however, stirred new interest in xenotransplantation. Arguments arose about the morality of taking the life of a primate to save the life of a human. Some people believe that animals raised for food, whose organs are not used as food, would be more suitable for organ supply. Pigs became the focus, because young pigs are roughly the same size and weight as humans.

At first, it did not appear that pig organ transplants would work, because human immune systems rapidly rejected pig organs. But with the advent of molecular biology, a new technique has been developed. By injecting a fertilized egg from the womb of a female pig with altered genes, scientists can produce piglets bearing a human gene called a DAF transgene. The scientists have begun to breed pigs whose organs will not be rejected by human immune systems. The work on xenotransplantation is ongoing and holds promise for the future.

At the same time that some doctors were working on animal transplantation, others were developing machines to replace organs. The goal, again, was to avoid organ rejection by the immune system. The mechanical organs would be made from non-antigenic materials such as Gore-Tex, a kind of plastic.

At the University of Utah, Dr. Robert Jarvik developed an air-driven version of the human heart. This artificial heart worked well in animals. In 1982, a man named Barney Clark became the first recipient of an artificial heart. Clark was over 60 years old and suffered from severe heart disease. He was told he had only a short time to live. Because of his age and failing health, he was turned down for a human heart transplant.

The operation to remove his heart and install the Jarvik heart was performed on December 1, 1982. Part of the artificial heart was implanted and another part was hooked to machines he carried with him. Although there were technical problems with this first machine, Clark survived for almost four months after the operation.

Clark, a retired dentist, was well aware that this experiment would probably not save his life, only extend it. Although he was often in great pain from the operations, he knew that by offering himself as an experimental "guinea pig," he was helping advance medical knowledge. In the end, he said, "It's been a pleasure to be able to help people." Since then, other patients have received Jarvik hearts. Some lived as long as two years after the operation. At each stage, more is learned.

Dr. Ernest Wynder once said, "It should be the function of medicine to have people die young—as late as possible." Techniques to enhance our immune systems may help make this possible.

GLOSSARY

adrenaline—another name for epinephrine, a hormone released by the adrenal gland during times of stress

AIDS—acquired immune deficiency syndrome; a disease caused by the human immunodeficiency virus (HIV), which attacks and destroys the helper T cells of the immune system

allergen—any antigen that produces an allergy or allergic immune response

allergy—a specialized immune response to an environmental, food, or chemical allergen. Most allergies happen when IgE antibodies react with the allergen and bind to mast cells and basophils. Hay fever is a common allergy.

amino acids—molecules containing carbon, hydrogen, oxygen, and nitrogen that are the fundamental building blocks of protein molecules.

antibodies—Y-shaped molecular proteins that attack and destroy specific microbes that invade the body

anti-antibodies—protein units that latch onto antibodies and stop them from interacting with an antigen, or invader. Anti-antibodies also react with specific B cells to induce immune responses.

antigen—any substance that causes an immune reaction in the body

autoimmune diseases—diseases caused by one's immune system attacking one's own tissues and cells

autoimmunity—misdirection of the immune system so that it turns against your own body

bacteria—single-celled living organisms

basophils—histamine-filled cells that circulate throughout the body; along with mast cells, they produce the symptoms of an allergy.

B cells—white blood cells that produce the antibody immune response; they turn into plasma cells, which make antibodies.

cellular (or cell-mediated) immunity—the function of the immune system that involves the T-cell response

complement—accessory proteins of the immune system that help antibodies kill invaders and signal other cells to the "battlefield" to clean up

cytokines—chemical messengers of the immune system, linking the brain and the immune system

delayed hypersensitivity—an allergic reaction that does not appear for several days, such as the rash caused by poison ivy

enzymes—proteins that help or drive chemical reactions in the body

epinephrine—a hormone released by the adrenal gland during times of stress

fungi—parasitic plants that live on or in the body

gamma globulin—the part of blood that contains most of the circulating antibodies

helper T cells—T cells that help control immune system function by sending other immune units to fight an invader

histocompatibility antigen—series of molecules displayed on the surface of cells that serve as a kind of ID badge

HIV—human immunodeficiency virus; the virus that causes the disease AIDS by destroying helper T cells

hormones—chemical messengers of the body

humoral immunity—the function of the immune system that involves the B-cell response. Also called antibody-mediated immunity.

hypersensitive reaction—an overreaction of the immune system to a foreign allergen; also called an *allergic* reaction.

hypersensitivity—overreaction of the immune system to a foreign allergen

hypothalamus—the thumbnail-sized nerve center in the brain that controls the pituitary gland and the nerve centers, which in turn control sleep, body temperature, sex, hunger, fear, and anger

immune—protected from disease

immune system—the units of the body, especially white blood cells, that work together to fight disease

immunity—protection from disease

immunodeficiency—a defect or weakness in the immune system because part or all of it was missing at birth or it has broken down

Immunoglobulin E (IgE)—the antibodies that bind to mast cells and basophils to produce allergic reactions

Immunoglobulin G (IgG)—the most common type of antibody

immunologist—a scientist who studies the immune system

interferons—chemicals produced by several different cells, including lymphocytes, in response to an attack by a virus

killer T cells—T cells that attack and destroy body invaders; also known as *effector cells*

leukocytes—a general name for all white blood cells

lymph—the protein-rich fluid in which white blood cells flow around the body

lymph nodes—small glands located at the juncture of lymph vessels, particularly in the neck, armpits, and groin. Lymph nodes are a major part of the immune system, developing and storing white blood cells and filtering bacteria.

lymphocytes—a subtype of leukocytes and the main cells of the immune system

lymph vessels—the channels that carry lymph fluid around the body

macrophages—from the Greek word meaning "big eater," white blood cells that form part of the first line of defense, attacking all foreign invaders and carrying parts of the invader back to the T cells. Macrophages also help clean up after the invaders are destroyed.

mast cells—histamine-filled cells that remain in the tissues. Along with basophils, they produce the symptoms of an allergy.

microbes—living organisms that are invisible except under a microscope

natural killer (NK) cells—T cells that attack body invaders

nucleic acid (DNA or RNA)—the molecules found in all cells that carry hereditary information and direct the activity of the cells

parasites—organisms that live in or on another organism

peptide—amino acid molecules bound together

phagocytes—immune system cells that help clean up after a battle with an invader

pituitary gland—the master gland that controls other hormone-producing glands and most hormones

plasma cells—B cells that have begun manufacturing antibodies

polymorphonuclear cells (polys)—specialized leukocytes that are part of the nonspecific front line of defense. They also help clean up after a battle.

polypeptide—peptides joined together to form the basic molecules of a protein

protein—molecules made up of amino acids. Proteins are necessary in all living matter and are the essential compound of the immune system.

protozoa—one-celled parasites

psychoneuroimmunology—the study of communication between the brain and the immune system and the ways in which immune functions are affected by thoughts

stem cells—cells in bone marrow that produce red blood cells, platelets, and white blood cells

steroids—chemicals that are made in the adrenal gland and act to suppress the immune system

suppressor T cells—T cells that help control immune system function by holding back immune units from fighting an invader, keeping a balance with the helper cells

T cells—white blood cells that are responsible for cell-mediated immune responses; they also act as general killer cells and control various immune functions.

thymus—a gland under the breastbone that helps in the development of the immune system

vaccination—receiving a shot of vaccine to be protected from a certain disease

vaccine—a preparation of killed or weakened microorganisms that will provide protection from a particular disease

virus—the smallest and simplest of all life forms

INDEX

ABOUT THE AUTHORS

Mark P. Friedlander, Jr., has been a trial attorney in Washington, D.C., and northern Virginia for over 40 years. Much of his legal work involves making complex scientific concepts accessible for laypeople. He is the author of several books, including *Winning the War Within*, a book on immunology for adults.

Dr. Terry M. Phillips, an immunologist for more than 20 years, is presently Director for the Analytical Immunochemistry Laboratories, which he founded in 1980, and Technical Director of the Immuno-oncology Laboratory, both at George Washington University Medical Center. From 1982 to 1992, he was Director of the Transplant Immunology Service, also at George Washington University Medical Center. He has participated in projects on cancer immunology, parasitology, and clinical immunology. His present work focuses on several areas of immunology, including studies on cytokine regulation of immunity, neuropeptide regulation of immunopathology and evolutionary immunology. He has collaborated with other investigators in Europe, the United States, Canada and Japan and has authored 250 scientific articles and two books on immunology.

PHOTO ACKNOWLEDGMENTS

The photographs and illustrations in this book are reproduced courtesy of: p. 2, © CNRI/S.P.L./Photo Researchers, Inc.; p. 6, Zeva Oelbaum/Peter Arnold, Inc.; p. 8, © National Cancer Institute S.P.L./Photo Researchers, Inc.; p. 9, © Oliver Meckes/Photo Researchers, Inc.; p. 12, © Bruce Ayers/Tony Stone Images; pp. 14, 21, 24, 49, 58, 76, Chris Gorecki; pp. 17, 38, Manfred Kage/Peter Arnold, Inc.; p. 19, © Meckes/Ottawa/Photo Researchers, Inc.; p. 33 (bottom), © NIBSC/S.P.L./Photo Researchers, Inc.; p. 25, © Prof. P. Motta/Department of Anatomy/University "La Sapienza," Rome/S.P.L./Photo Researchers, Inc.; p. 30, © Oliver Meckes/Gelderblom/Photo Researchers, Inc.; p. 33 (top), © National Institute of Health/S.P.L./Photo Researchers, Inc.; p. 35, © Science Source/Photo Researchers, Inc.; p. 36, © Andrew Syred/Tony Stone Images; pp. 40, 42, Corbis-Bettmann; p. 46 (top), 102, UPI/Corbis-Bettmann; p. 46 (bottom), Archive Photos; p. 51, Science VU/Visuals Unlimited; p. 52, © David Hanover/Tony Stone Images; pp. 56, 60, 62, 65, National Cancer Institute; p. 70, © Robert Torrez/Tony Stone Images; p. 79, © James Darell/Tony Stone Images; p. 81, © Barbara Filet/Tony Stone Images; p. 82, © Scott Camazine/Photo Researchers, Inc.; pp. 84, 90, David Scharf/Peter Arnold, Inc.; p. 87, © Secchi-Lecaque/Roussel-UCLAF/CNRI/S.P.L./Photo Researchers, Inc.; p. 92, © Lawrence Migdale/Tony Stone Images; p. 94, © NASA/Science Source/Photo Researchers, Inc.; p. 97, Comstock Inc.; p. 100, © James King-Holmes/S.P.L./Photo Researchers, Inc.

Front cover photograph National Cancer Institute/S.P.L./Photo Researchers, Inc.